POSTMODERNITY

KEY IDEAS
Series Editor: Peter Hamilton
The Open University

KEY IDEAS

Series Editor: PETER HAMILTON
The Open University, Milton Keynes

Designed to complement the successful *Key Sociologists*, this series covers the main concepts, issues, debates, and controversies in sociology and the social sciences. The series aims to provide authoritative essays on central topics of social science, such as community, power, work, sexuality, inequality, benefits and ideology, class, family, etc. Books adopt a strong individual 'line' constituting original essays rather than literary surveys, and form lively and original treatments of their subject matter. The books will be useful to students and teachers of sociology, political science, economics, psychology, philosophy, and geography.

THE SYMBOLIC CONSTRUCTION OF COMMUNITY
ANTHONY P. COHEN, Department of Social Anthropology, University of Manchester
SOCIETY
DAVID FRISBY and DEREK SAYER, Department of Sociology, University of Glasgow
SEXUALITY
JEFFREY WEEKS, Social Work Studies Department, University of Southampton
WORKING
GRAEME SALAMAN, Faculty of Social Sciences, The Open University, Milton Keynes
BELIEFS AND IDEOLOGY
KENNETH THOMPSON, Faculty of Social Sciences, The Open University, Milton Keynes
EQUALITY
BRYAN TURNER, School of Social Sciences, The Flinders University of South Australia
HEGEMONY
ROBERT BOCOCK, Faculty of Social Sciences, The Open University, Milton Keynes
RACISM
ROBERT MILES, Department of Sociology, University of Glasgow

POSTMODERNITY

BARRY SMART

London and New York

First published in 1993
by Routledge
11 New Fetter Lane, London EC4P 4EE

Simultaneously published in the USA and Canada
by Routledge
29 West 35th Street, New York, NY 10001

Reprinted 1993

Typeset in Times by Intype, London
Printed and bound in Great Britain by Clays Ltd, St Ives plc

British Library Cataloguing in Publication Data
A catalogue record for this book is available from the British
Library.

Library of Congress Cataloging in Publication Data
Smart, Barry.
    Postmodernity / Barry Smart.
        p.   cm.— (Key ideas series)
    Includes bibliographical references and index.
    1. Postmodernism—Social aspects.   I. Title.   II. Series.
    HM73.S585   1992   92–9969
    303.4–dc20   CIP

    ISBN 0–415–06961–0

What are we calling post-modernity? . . . I must say that I have trouble answering this . . . because I've never clearly understood what was meant . . . by the word 'modernity'.

Michel Foucault

Is this the sense in which we are not modern? Incommensurability, heterogeneity . . . the absence of a supreme tribunal? Or, on the other hand, is this the continuation of romanticism, the nostalgia that accompanies the retreat of . . . etc? Nihilism? A well executed work of mourning for Being? And the hope that is born with it? Which is still the hope of redemption? With all of this still remaining inscribed within the thought of a redemptive future? Could it be that 'we' are no longer telling ourselves anything? Are 'we' not telling, whether bitterly or gladly, the great narrative of the end of great narratives? For thought to remain modern, doesn't it suffice that it think in terms of the end of some history? Or, is postmodernity the pastime of an old man who scrounges in the garbage-heap of finality looking for leftovers, who brandishes unconsciousnesses, lapses, limits, confines, goulags, parataxes, non-senses, or paradoxes, and who turns this into the glory of his novelty, into his promise of change?

Jean-François Lyotard

I occasionally get just as tired of the slogan of 'postmodernism' as anyone else, but when I am tempted to regret my complicity with it, to deplore its misuses and its notoriety, and to conclude with some reluctance that it caused more problems than it solves, I find myself pausing to wonder whether any other concept can dramatise the issue in quite so effective and economical a fashion.

Frederic Jameson

Contents

Acknowledgements

Earlier versions of Chapters 3, 4 and 5 were presented at the XII World Congress of Sociology on 'Sociology for One World: Unity and Diversity' (Madrid 1990), the Thesis Eleven international conference on 'Reason and Imagination in Modern Culture' (Melbourne 1991), and the annual conference of the American Sociological Association on 'The World of Ethnic Relations' (Cincinnati 1991) respectively. I would like to thank participants for their suggestions and criticisms, for drawing attention to elements of my argument that were in need of clarification and reformulation, even if I might not have seemed appreciative at the time!

Versions of Chapters 2 and 3 have appeared in *Sociology* (1990) and *Thesis Eleven* (1991) respectively and I would like to thank the editors and anonymous referees for their helpful comments and suggestions.

Once again Chris Rojek deserves my thanks for encouraging me to proceed with the book, as does Kym Fullerton for her fast and efficient preparation of the manuscript.

Finally, a personal note of gratitude to Jo Burgin for tolerating my unsociable working hours, helping with the proofs, and much else besides.

1

New times, old troubles

INTRODUCTION

Postmodernity is a controversial term, a term that elicits highly charged reactions across intellectual disciplines and associated theoretical and political constituencies. Postmodernity is an issue in anthropology, sociology, philosophy, geography, theological studies, literary criticism and economics to mention only a few areas. Neo-conservative social analysts, critical theorists, classical and not-so-classical Marxists, rational-choice sociologists and standpoint feminists seem at times to share common cause in criticising the very idea of postmodernity. An equally heterogeneous collection of analysts and commentators have embraced the term. What is it that has aroused so much attention; precipitated eager acceptance and yet called forth so much bile and scorn; pleased or troubled so many who seem so secure in their convictions? Could it be that such very mixed reactions to the nebulous notion of postmodernity betray traces of the very conditions to which the term tentatively and not a little ambiguously refers? Reactions to the issues raised under the contentious signs of 'postmodernity', 'postmodernism' and the 'postmodern' are rarely sober, measured or thoughtful. All too frequently post-modernity is presented as a condition to embrace, to celebrate and promote, or equally problematically set up as that which needs to be criticised, dismissed or rejected (Lash 1990: 2).

Postmodernity. What is it? What was it? When was it? Were you there? Amused? Bemused? Convinced? Disdainful? Enchanted? Irritated or just plain indifferent? For some, the grazers and zappers of the analytic domain, it is already a question of what postmodernity *was*. The answer a period extending from the mid-1970s to the late 1980s when disillusionment with the prospects for radical political strategy appeared to be extensive and neo-conservative reaction and neo-liberal economic policy held sway. References to post-postmodernity suggest it is a time already past. Postmodernity no longer a novelty, no longer fashionable, simply a bore now that everybody is doing it. More interesting in my view are the contributions which consider post-modernity to be a matter of current concern, an idea that may have a bearing on our understanding and experience of present conditions. Postmodernity as a contemporary social, cultural and political condition. Postmodernity as a form of life, a form of reflection upon and a response to the accumulating signs of the limits and limitations of modernity. Postmodernity as a way of living with the doubts, uncertainties and anxieties which seem increasingly to be a corollary of modernity, the inescapable price to be paid for the gains, the benefits and the pleasures, associated with modernity. In the latter set of comments there is the implication of postmodernity as a condition necessarily closely articulated with modernity, postmodernity as modernity in its nascent state perhaps, or postmodernity as a more modest modernity, a sign of modernity having come to terms with its own limits and limitations. An alternative, radically different conception, introduced by Giddens (1990), presents postmodernity as a form of life 'beyond modernity'. Postmodernity as a possible social future, a condition, a form of life that has yet to be realised, an alternative form of sociality that can only emerge after we have settled our accounts with modernity, have succeeded in extricating ourselves from the remorseless spirals of flux, turmoil and perpetual transformation that seem to be intrinsic to modernity. The key features attributed to postmodernity as a future-oriented project include a post-scarcity order; multilayered democratic participation; demilitarisation; and a humanisation of technology (Giddens 1990: 164). Postmodernity in this instance is very much *post*modernity. It represents an example of the reconstitution of utopian thought.

Postmodernity is certainly a highly loaded term. So much comment has already been placed in circulation about the contentious idea of postmodernity that it is difficult to avoid having a view on the issues raised. Hard not to have committed oneself 'for' or 'against' or to simply be tired of the whole business. For some analysts reference to postmodernity is tantamount to mentioning the unmentionable, articulating the unacceptable, the indefensible, the inconceivable. To invoke the relevance of a notion of postmodernity is to be found guilty of misreading the signs, identifying the 'different', if not the 'new', when attention should instead have been directed to exploring what are considered to be variations on or of the same, in short aspects of modernity and its continuing complex development. In contrast to contributions which argue that postmodernity is a redundant term, inappropriate and/or unnecessary for understanding contemporary social, cultural and political conditions, there are a growing number of analyses which identify aspects of the circumstances we encounter, the experiences we share, and the difficulties we confront, as 'postmodern', in other words as not reducible simply to a preexisting and/or evolving modernity. My discussion of postmodernity will be directed for the most part to the latter category of analyses, to contributions which consider the introduction of a concept of postmodernity appropriate and necessary for understanding current conditions. But since I am not a convert I will continue to draw upon some of the more critical analyses.

As I have implied above a concept of postmodernity has been invoked to describe developments in a number of areas, including architecture, art, literature, cinema, music, fashion, communications, experiences of space and time, aspects of identity, and sexuality, as well as philosophical, political and sociological reflections on the same and broader questions of social life. Interior and exterior designs, various popular cultural communications, commodities and texts, for example films, records, television advertisements and magazines, 'new' social and political movements, the erosion of cultural hierarchies, questioning of epistemological foundations and metanarratives, as well as concerns about new miniaturised technologies, the proliferation of shopping malls and consumer culture, and complex forms of articulation between the global and the local have all been described as postmodern. But then you probably know that already. How could you not? You will have read some of the novels, *The Satanic Verses*, *Foucault's Pendulum*, seen some of the films, *Blue Velvet*, *Blade Runner*, *Brazil*, watched the series *Twin Peaks* on television, listened to the music and watched the videos of bands like Talking Heads, flicked through magazines such as *The Face* and *I-D*, admired or laughed at the furniture and perhaps sat on a Memphis chair, viewed with amazement and perhaps not a little incredulity the wonders of 'Officina Alessi' products and appliances for making tea, coffee and other culinary delights, stood inside or outside architectural structures like the AT & T building in New York, or seen the photographs in glossy, expensive texts, wondered about Warhol's painting *Diamond Dust Shoes*, and probably have confronted, perhaps taken an interest in, dropped, or embraced some of the social, cultural, political and philosophical analyses that have sought to condemn, celebrate, or critically and sensitively explore the various complex and diverse manifestations that float around in the cloudy constellation of the postmodern.

NEW TIMES?

The idea that we are living in new times is interesting, persuasive, if not seductive, particularly in a cultural context where there has been, for some time now, a cult of the new, a social and economic context in which innovation and novelty have been promoted, their virtues extolled, often through implied associations with ideas of progress and/or development. Moreover, on a number of fronts there do appear to be signs of significant forms of change permeating social, economic, political and cultural institutions and practices. Such signs have undoubtedly lent credence to the idea of new times. But if there is a sense in which it is hard to dispute the existence of significant processes of transformation affecting our experiences of everyday life, economic activity, political association, and cultural production and consumption, it is important to guard against a too hasty acceptance of the idea that everything has changed, or, at least, all that matters has. Whilst it would be foolish to dispute the existence of changed and, for that matter, changing circumstances, it is appropriate, indeed necessary, to be aware, and to beware, of the things which may not have changed, the continuities with the past which remain, or perhaps have been reinvigorated, the conditions which have prevailed.

There may indeed be respects in which we are living in new times, or more cautiously and modestly, living in an interregnum. Our present era may, in some important respects, stand in a relationship of discontinuity with the past, yet amidst the differences there remain familiar traces, signs of continuity. We may be living in different conditions but many of the circumstances we encounter and experiences we share, both the problems and the pleasures, may be longer-standing and more familiar than a notion of new times seems to allow. In short if we are living in new times we also appear to be encountering old troubles, familiar possibilities and pleasures.

The idea that we might be living in new times, or be on the verge of experiencing such times, is itself by no means a new one. The pronouncement of new times seems to be a recurring feature of modernity. Indeed it has been argued that the very idea of the modern has served to express 'the consciousness of an epoch that related itself to the past . . . in order to view itself as the result of a transition from the old to the new' (Habermas 1981: 3). A notion of the modern, albeit with varying content, is considered to have been around since the late fifth century and to have been particularly prominent in the late seventeenth-century *querelle des anciens et des modernes* which brought the blind veneration accorded to classical antiquity to a close and led to the cultivation of a sense of modernity as a distinctive and superior form of life (Smart 1990). However, the association of new times with modernity is by no means uncontroversial. The equation of new times with modernity is disturbed in the first instance by a range of different and at times conflicting views taken on the subject of modern conditions and in a second instance by the increasing attention accorded to the troubling figure of postmodernity, a condition which has been described as signifying a qualitative transformation of modernity. Moreover, just as the concept of modernity is the subject of disagreement, there being a range of different views as to when the modern era commenced and what its principal features might be considered to include, so the idea of postmodernity has proven to be controversial and elusive. Clarification of the matters in dispute is not helped by the fact that some of the key terms in play in the debate over new times, namely modernity, modernism, postmodernity and postmodernism, are closely connected and in consequence difficult to distinguish and disentangle from each other.

There have been several attempts to provide a degree of clarification of the complex issues associated with the ambiguous notions of modernism, modernity, postmodernism and postmodernity (Huyssen 1984; Foster 1985; Featherstone 1988; Turner 1990; Boyne and Rattansi 1990). Although there are some differences between contributors over questions of historical trajectory as well as the features, figures and texts considered to exemplify modern and postmodern forms, and their respective differences, there appears to be a shared sense that significant cultural transformations have been taking place in Western societies during the period since the end of the second world war and further that the term 'postmodernism' may be appropriate, for the time being at least, to describe some of the implied shifts in 'sensibility, practices and discourse formations' (Huyssen 1984: 8). The seemingly related term of 'postmodernity' is employed more broadly, and ambitiously in some cases, to refer to the possible emergence of a different historical condition, to suggest that the cultural configuration of postmodernism may itself be a constitutive element of a larger socioeconomic and political constellation (e.g. Boyne and Rattansi 1990: 9). When we turn to consider in more detail the question of the relationship between postmodernism and postmodernity and their respective modern roots or equivalents it becomes evident that there are three possible alternative positions to which analysts have been drawn (Huyssen 1984: 10).

Postmodernism may be described as a cultural configuration that is broadly continuous with modernism, that is as not significantly different. One implication of which is the superficiality, if not redundancy of the term, for it simply attempts to fabricate differences within the same. As Featherstone argues many of the features considered to be intrinsic to modernism, 'aesthetic self-consciousness and reflexiveness; a rejection of narrative structure in favour of simultaneity and montage; an exploration of the paradoxical, ambiguous and uncertain open-ended nature of reality; and a rejection of the notion of an integrated personality in favour of an emphasis upon the destructured, dehumanised subject . . . are appropriated into various definitions of postmodernism' (1988: 202). An understandable response to which is scepticism concerning the claims made that postmodernism identifies something significantly different from modernism. In contrast to the notion that postmodernism is in important respects continuous with modernism, a second position favoured by some analysts suggests more of a radical rupture between the two. As Jameson remarks in his seminal essay on the cultural logic of late capitalism, 'even if all the constitutive features of postmodernism were identical and continuous with those of an older modernism – a position I feel to be demonstrably erroneous . . . the two phenomena would still remain utterly distinct in their meaning and social function' (1984: 57). The distinctive features attributed by Jameson to postmodernism include the following: a new depthlessness and a consequent weakening of historicity; the 'waning of affect'; a fragmentation of the subject; the omnipresence of pastiche and prevalence of a 'nostalgia mode'; and the breakdown of the signifying chain following the collapse of the referent and associated crisis of representation. Postmodernism is said to be a 'culture increasingly dominated by space and spatial logic' (1984: 71), a cultural configuration which is constituted in and through complex relationships with a new generation of technologies, which themselves are articulated with the emergence of a new global economic formation.

What emerges from Jameson's work is the sense that the three episodes in the development of the capitalist mode of production and their respective technological corollaries, schematically outlined by Mandel (1980), are closely articulated with forms of cultural periodisation. The three fundamental stages identified in the development of capitalism, namely market, monopoly and multi-national forms, closely articulated with particular revolutions in the machine production of technologies (e.g. steam-driven motors; electric and combustion motors; electronic and nuclear-powered apparatuses), are described by Jameson as confirming his own 'cultural periodisation of the stages of realism, modernism and postmodernism' (Jameson 1984: 78). It is possible to detect here the distant echo of Marx's *1859 Preface* concerning the mode of production of material life and its conditioning of social, political and intellectual life in general. But whilst there is an admission of the need to approach the question of postmodernism through a consideration of the 'world of late capitalism' something more than an endorsement of the determined and/or relatively autonomous status of culture is at stake. The claim made by Jameson is that we are witnessing 'a prodigious expansion of culture throughout the social realm, to the point at which everything in our social life – from economic value and state power to practices and to the very structure of the psyche itself – can be said to have become "cultural" in some original and as yet untheorised sense' (1984: 87). Culture has become all-pervasive and postmodernism has become the 'cultural dominant'. In brief the impression is conveyed that we are indeed living in new times. A conclusion which has provoked a good deal of criticism from fellow travellers (Callinicos 1989).

A comparable conception of postmodernism as signifying a break with modernism is developed in an analysis of the visual arts by Burgin (1986). In this instance postmodernism is considered to provide 'our first glimpse of the historical emergence of a field of *post*-Romantic aesthetics', to signify the end of a series of interdependent discursive forms 'which began in the Enlightenment and culminated in the recent period of "high modernism" ' (1986: 204). In contrast to analyses which invoke notions of continuity or a break between postmodernism and modernism there are a number of other contributions which approach the two configurations in relational terms, which keep in mind the relational character of postmodernism, the inescapable etymological proximity of the term to modernism (Huyssen 1984; Lyotard 1986, 1989; Newman 1989). Postmodernism in this third, relational sense becomes a way of describing a broad range of aesthetic, literary, and cultural responses to modernism, a longstanding series of engagements with modernism, early signs of which have been traced back to the late nineteenth century and the work of Nietzsche, and subsequently the philosophy of Heidegger. For example, Habermas (1987) criticises Nietzsche for preparing an entry into postmodern preoccupations, for opening up paths subsequently 'travelled by Heidegger and Bataille'. Vattimo (1988) also recognises the affinity between Nietzsche, Heidegger and contemporary deliberations over postmodernism, but unlike Habermas he appears more comfortable with the possibility that we are living in 'the era of the end of metaphysics' (1988: 106), and goes on to argue that in the arts and philosophy there is a sense in which we have already taken leave of modernity. This remains a controversial matter, as I hope will become clear from my discussion.

Although the philosophical roots of postmodernism may be traced to the late nineteenth century the term itself really only began to be employed from the 1930s. An early reference occurs in the contribution to literary criticism of Federico de Onis who uses the term *postmodernismo* to describe a 'kind of exhausted and mildly conservative *modernismo*' (Calinescu 1977: 133). A comparable use of the term occurs in the late 1950s in America to lament the exhaustion of the modern movement, to describe the growing signs of modernism's denouement and the emergence of a new sensibility. However, it was the mid-1970s before the term began to be more widely employed, in relation to architecture, dance, painting, film and music.

> [By the] early 1980s the modernism/postmodernism constellation in the arts and the modernity/postmodernity constellation in social theory had become one of the most contested terrains in the intellectual life of Western societies. And the terrain is contested precisely because there is so much more at stake than the existence or non-existence of a new artistic style, so much more also than just the 'correct' theoretical line.
>
> (Huyssen 1984: 12)

Moreover the terrain continues to be contested even though we are all becoming weary, very weary, of the fads and foibles, not to mention the knee-jerk reflexes, which the issues involved seem to have attracted.

Postmodernism became more prominent in America in the course of the 1960s, constituted as a potentially avantgardist cultural configuration distinguished by four key characteristics:

(i) future oriented, innovative temporal imagination;
(ii) iconoclastic attack on the institution, organisation and ideology of art;
(iii) technological optimism, bordering at times on euphoria; and
(iv) promotion of 'popular culture' as a challenge to 'high art'.

Huyssen describes these features of early American postmodernism as effectively the 'prehistory of the postmodern', ultimately because the avantgardist aims and ambitions could not be sustained. Not unlike the high modernism which it saw as incorporated and codified, avantgarde postmodernism had exhausted its potential by the 1970s, if not played out the 'endgame of international avantgardism' (Huyssen 1984: 24). It is in this context that we find disagreement developing around the idea of postmodernism, notably between analysts and critics who conceive of postmodernism as a culture of eclecticism which celebrates the status quo, and those who argue that there is an alternative postmodernism 'which seeks to deconstruct modernism and resist the status quo' (Foster 1985: xii). In short a contrast between an affirmative and a critical postmodernism, or a 'postmodernism of reaction' and a 'postmodernism of resistance'.

If postmodernism first became an issue in America it is now very much a part of the European scene. And if there was an initial sense that perhaps Habermas (1981) was correct in conceiving of postmodernism as simply a 'neoconservative' tendency within art and philosophy, that no longer seems to be the way analysts interested in generating critical analyses and developing radical political strategies see things. For example, a number of analysts working out of a Marxist problematic and interested in developing forms of inquiry and political strategies relevant to current conditions have embraced a critical postmodernism (Laclau and Mouffe 1985; Laclau 1988, 1990; Soja 1989), as have feminists who wish to avoid the problems which arise from attempting to 'oppose the discourses of male domination by appealing to a metanarrative of universal justice and freedom' (Hekman 1990: 187). Of course there are still critics for whom postmodernism constitutes something like heresy and the term continues to both evade specification and attract controversy.

POSTSTRUCTURALISM AND POSTMODERNISM

A common reference made in discussions of postmodernism is to a diverse set of initiatives in French social and philosophical thought generally identified with the respective works of some, if not all, of the following: Baudrillard, Deleuze, Derrida, Foucault, Guattari, Lacan and Lyotard. As different as the analyses of the aforementioned figures are in a number of significant respects, they have each been identified as contributors to another problematically constituted 'unity' known as poststructuralism (Giddens 1987; Dews 1987; Poster 1990). Specifically it is argued that the respective works of the analysts identified above call attention and contribute to the 'crisis of representation' evident in epistemological, artistic, and political contexts (Boyne and Rattansi 1990: 13); reveal the fragile and problematic representational character of language, the disarticulation of words and things, and the ways in which meaning is increasingly 'sustained through mechanisms of self-referentiality' (Poster 1990:

13); and thereby deny 'us any access to an independent reality' (Callinicos 1990: 101); and last, but by no means least, present the subject as 'fragmented and decentred in the social field' undermining, as a result, the notion of 'identity as a fixed and unified phenomenon' (Sawicki 1988: 174). As such the collection of positions and analyses brought together under the appellation 'poststructuralism' are considered to have contributed to the constitution of postmodernism. But if particular contributions to social and philosophical thought collected together under the sign of poststructuralism have been an element in deliberations over the question of the postmodern, it is necessary to remember that postmodernism and poststructuralism are not identical. Indeed it may be argued that

> poststructuralism is primarily a discourse of and about modernism . . . [and that] we must begin to entertain the notion that rather than offering a *theory of postmodernity* and developing an analysis of contemporary culture, French theory provides us primarily with an *archaeology of modernity*, a theory of modernism at the stage of its exhaustion.
>
> (Huyssen 1984: 39)

In brief, an analysis of the limits and limitations of modernism, its tarnished ambitions, unfulfilled promises, and the dilemmas that follow from facing up to the loss of the vision of redemption through art, literature and culture. However, in so far as the various analyses subsumed within poststructuralism provide a retrospective theoretical reading of modernism it is not difficult to understand how poststructuralism has become conflated with a relational sense of postmodernism. But whilst we might understand what has happened, the confusions, conflations and over-extensions which exist in connection with the question of the relationship between poststructuralism and postmodernism remain a problem.

There have been a number of attempts to clarify the question of the relationship between poststructuralism and postmodernism. It has been suggested that there is an 'affiliation of poststructuralist theories of desire with . . . postmodern currents' (Lash 1990: 118) and that both 'textualist' (à la Derrida) and 'worldly' (à la Foucault) strands of poststructuralist thought have given 'conceptual expression to the themes explored by contemporary artists' (Callinicos 1990: 2), and thereby contributed significantly to the constitution of postmodernism. In marked contrast to the tendency to equate, if not conflate, poststructuralism and postmodernism Huyssen describes poststructuralism as offering a theory of modernism and as attempting to 'salvage aesthetic modernism for the late 20th century' (1984: 40). Furthermore, such textualist and aestheticising preoccupations associated with poststructuralism are compared unfavourably with alternative postmodern responses. For example, poststructuralism is criticised for duplicating 'on the level of aesthetics and theory what capitalism as a system of exchange relations produces tendentially in everyday life: the denial of subjectivity in the very process of its construction' (Huyssen 1984: 44). The implication is that questions of subjectivity and authorship are squarely on the postmodern agenda, even if they are decidedly absent from the poststructuralist text. In short Huyssen argues for a 'fundamental non-identity' between poststructuralism and postmodernism.

Responding to the lack of conceptual coherence associated with postmodernism, Boyne and Rattansi, at one level at least, endorse Huyssen's view by expressing criticism of the overextension of the term, beyond particular aesthetic and cultural projects, to encompass 'poststructuralist work in literary theory, philosophy and history (Derrida, Foucault, Lyotard), Rorty's form of pragmatist philosophy, post-positivist philosophy of science (Kuhn, Feyerabend) [and] the textual movement in cultural anthropology (Clifford, Marcus)' (1990: 10). But unlike Huyssen they consider the overextension to already be a *fait accompli*, an established element in the debate over contemporary conditions, and as such consider it legitimate to employ postmodernism 'broadly to include discussions of . . . poststructuralism in literary theory, philosophy and historical and social analysis' (1990: 11). This represents an understandable compromise, a realistic response to, or recognition of, the way the debate over postmodernism has developed. It also suggests the possibility of some, albeit small, relief from the proliferating 'posts' – postmodernism, poststructuralism, postindustrialism, postfeminism, postmarxism etc. (Bell 1973) – by implying that perhaps the fabricated unity of poststructuralism can be marginalised, if not abandoned to the postmodern mice. After all analysts seem to have had virtually as much difficulty differentiating between the various versions of structuralism and poststructuralism as they have had distinguishing between aspects of modernism and postmodernism. On that somewhat jaundiced note I want to shift the focus from postmodernism *per se* to the related notion of postmodernity.

POSTMODERNITY

Analyses of postmodernism generally allude to or invoke some sense of a broader context within which postmodern cultural forms and practices are considered to have emerged and developed. References abound to 'political, social and cultural constellations' (Huyssen 1984: 52) and 'a social, political and cultural configuration' (Boyne and Rattansi 1990: 9), as well as to the broader notion of an 'epochal shift or break from modernity involving the emergence of a new social totality with its own distinct organising principles' (Featherstone 1988: 198). In some cases specific socioeconomic and technological factors and processes are prioritised and reference is made to the emergence of a postindustrial society or age (Bell 1976), in others comparable transformations are considered to be symptoms of further developments in the capitalist mode of production towards 'late' (Jameson 1984), 'disorganised' (Lash and Urry 1987) or 'flexible accumulation' (Harvey 1989) forms. In turn reference may be made to a notion of *post*modernity. However, the concept of postmodernity is introduced not only to imply the existence of a distinctive configuration, a new epoch or age, but also to describe the development of a relatively novel 'condition' or 'mood' which both shapes and is increasingly expressed in conduct and experience. In short, as with the concept of postmodernism, a concept of postmodernity is employed in three distinctive senses, namely to imply differences, but through a relationship of continuity with (capitalist) modernity, to indicate a break or rupture with modern conditions, or finally as a way of relating to modern forms of life, effectively a coming to terms, a facing up to modernity, its benefits and its problematic consequences, its limits and its limitations.

Let me continue my consideration by first of all disposing of one of the three possible senses of the term postmodernity noted above, namely the notion that we can locate a break with or from modernity, in effect identify the onset of a new era or epoch. I should add that I am not here alluding to the notion of 'new times' *per se*, although I recognise that one of the ways that term has been used signifies a break or rupture with the past. Examples of the introduction of a concept of the postmodern to signify a new historical era or period are provided in the respective works of Toynbee (1954a, 1954b) and Wright Mills (1970). Toynbee makes several references to a postmodern age in Western civilisation, by which he seems to mean a period which began 'at the turn of the nineteenth and twentieth centuries' (1954a: 338), a period in which an accelerating rate of technological change and the impact of associated innovations in the realm of human affairs has increasingly run ahead of slower more uneven transformations in the moral and political capacities of humanity. It might seem that Toynbee is genuinely concerned about our general capacity to cope with the scale, pace and moral and political impact of particular socioeconomic and technological changes. But it is clear that there is a more specific agenda in Toynbee's analysis, namely that the onset of a postmodern age is to be lamented principally because it disturbs the hegemony of the 'North-Western European middle class'. Unprecedentedly prosperous and comfortable, the middle classes, Toynbee argues, imagined history had reached its end, believed that their safe modern form of life had 'miraculously come to stay as a timeless present' (1954b: 421). The 'first postmodern general war', the first world war, its sequel and other socioeconomic, political and technological developments which followed the cessation of hostilities in 1945 are considered to have shattered middle-class complacency and contributed to a growing sense of crisis in Western civilisation. A comparable paranoia is exemplified by Daniel Bell who, two decades after Toynbee, expressed a similarly nostalgic conservative concern about the perils of the postmodern, in particular the cultural contradictions afflicting middle-class values and lifestyles in America (Smart 1992).

Forty years on Toynbee's worries about the threats to capitalism arising from a redirection of the creative energies of the middle class in Britain away from private enterprise and towards a growing public sphere seem, to say the least, unwarranted, misplaced, if not bizarre. As we witness the rolling back of what we have come to know as the welfare state; the increasing commodification of health, welfare and educational provision and concomitant promotion of the alleged virtues of the untrammelled market, business culture and entrepreneurship; the growth of conspicuous and not-so-conspicuous consumption on the back of a rising tide of debt; and the radical transformation of what used to be called the societies of 'actually existing socialism' (Bahro 1978) towards those 'Western' forms of economic and political organisation formerly regarded as anathema, Toynbee's postmodern scenario appears preposterous. One thing at least seems clear: our times, whether we describe them as new, postmodern, or whatever, are not Toynbee's times. Yet, having said that we need to be careful not to be taken in by all the noise being made about the end of history (again), a 'New World Order', and the triumph of capitalism (Fukuyama 1989).

Throughout Toynbee's comments on the onset of a postmodern age there is a sense that it is the prevalence of middleclass values and lifestyles that has constituted *modern* Western civilisation. The challenge to middle-class economic, political and cultural hegemony from within (by 'industrial workers') and from without (by 'Asiatic dominions' and 'new supranational Great Powers') is clearly viewed with regret by Toynbee, as is the possibility that the economic and political epicentre of Western civilisation has shifted across the Atlantic to America, the home, as Baudrillard idiosyncratically describes it, of 'the original version of modernity' (1988c: 76). With the rise of Japanese industrial and financial corporations, American hegemony in its turn has been placed in question, causing some analysts to argue that 'America is dead' (Wark 1990: 20) and to suggest that the epicentre has shifted once more to the Pacific Rim and the East. Perhaps that is what the preoccupation with postmodernity signifies, a geopolitical relocation of the creative, innovatory momentum associated with modernity beyond the West. As one analyst has remarked, '[i]f the postmodern has more than a flip significance then, it means a loss of mastery with its origins in the premature end of the American Century . . . the transfer of power away from America and its cosy satellites toward new centres' (Wark 1990: 20).

The second example of a periodising sense of the term postmodernity is implied in Wright Mills's late 1950s reflections on the collapse of liberalism and socialism 'as adequate explanations of the world and of ourselves' (1970: 184). Twenty years or more before Lyotard's pronouncement of the end of 'grand narratives' Wright Mills already sensed which way the wind was blowing. Drawing on Max Weber's critical reflections on modern forms of life and Adorno and Horkheimer's identification of the dark side of the dialectic of enlightenment Wright Mills identified the end of an epoch, 'the ending of what is called The Modern Age' and the beginning of a 'post-modern period' (Wright Mills 1970: 184). The new period of postmodernity is distinguished by an increasingly pervasive sense that modern assumptions about the intrinsic relation of reason and freedom can no longer be sustained. As Wright Mills observes, 'ideas of freedom and of reason have become moot . . . increased rationality may not be assumed to make for increased freedom' (1970: 185–6). But, as I have implied, the idea that processes of growing rationalisation do not necessarily produce progressive increases in freedom and human happiness is by no means recent or novel. To that extent talk of the end of modernity and advent of postmodernity as a new period or epoch is unconvincing. The issues identified by Wright Mills are interesting and important, but rather than signifying a new period or epoch they point instead to the steady accretion, the increasing pervasiveness of a mood or condition, a response to modernity that is relatively longstanding, one that has been gathering momentum since the end of the nineteenth century.

Although both Toynbee and Wright Mills introduce the idea of a new epoch or period it is clear that they approach the question of postmodernity in different ways and with quite different political agendas. Toynbee views the passing of liberal capitalism with a great deal of regret and clearly regards the growth of a public sphere and associated economic and political changes with grave concern. The implied dark vision is of 'postmodern' masses threatening to dissipate capitalism, challenge prevailing cultural hierarchies and in consequence undermine the core values of Western civilisation. The current debate over population migration into and within Europe seems to be replaying some of these themes and fears. Wright Mills is also concerned about the assumptions and values which have shaped Western civilisation, but the difference is that they are considered to be justifiably in question. Our explanations, assumptions and values, along with the grand narratives of liberalism and socialism which derive from that complex eighteenth-century configuration known as 'The Enlightenment', are found wanting when we try to make sense of contemporary conditions. As Wright Mills remarks, 'the ideals of reason and of freedom must now be restated as problems in more precise and solvable ways than have been available to earlier thinkers and investigators. For in our time these two values, reason and freedom, are in obvious yet subtle peril' (1970: 186). But rather than conceive of postmodernity as a period or epoch, the term might more appropriately be employed, as I have already indicated, to describe the

condition of recognition of that subtle peril, in effect to denote
a way of relating to the limits and limitations of modernity, a
way of living with the realisation that the promise of modernity
to deliver order, certainty and security will remain unfulfilled.
Facing up to this condition, recognising 'that certainty is not to
be, and yet [persevering] in the pursuit of knowledge born of
the determination to smother and weed out contingency'
(Bauman 1991a: 244) is how we might understand the notion of
postmodernity. It is this relational sense of postmodernity that
is central to my discussion in the following chapters.

Before turning to the respects in which the argument about
new times has been interrupted and subjected to question by the
persistence of old(er) troubles it is necessary to comment briefly
on a third way in which the notion of postmodernity has been
employed, namely to connote differences within a complex
relationship of continuity with a longer-standing modern socioeconomic formation, namely capitalism. In this instance a concept of postmodernity serves to describe distinctive features of
processes of transformation occurring within contemporary capitalism. For example:

> accelerations in turnover times, in production, exchange,
> and consumption . . . . [as well as the] rapidity with
> which currency markets fluctuate across the world's
> spaces, the extraordinary power of money capital flow
> in what is now a global stock and financial market, and
> the volatility of what the purchasing power of money
> might represent, define . . . a high point of that highly
> problematic intersection of money, time and space as
> interlocking elements of social power in the political
> economy of postmodernity.
>
> (Harvey 1989: 291, and 298)

In this instance the notion of postmodernity is employed to
describe the latest phase of time-space compression which itself
constitutes a part of ongoing procedures of capitalist modernisation. It is important to emphasise that the differences identified
by Harvey, and described by the notion of postmodernity, are
not considered to signify any 'fundamental *change* of social condition' (1989: 111). It is also worth adding that at times postmodernism and postmodernity are employed virtually as synonyms
(1989: 327–8, 338–42), a confusing conflation to which analysis
in this area is vulnerable. What is clear from Harvey's wide-

ranging and careful exploration of the condition of postmodernity is that there are significant differences emerging to which we need to attend, but that, in the final analysis, such differences can be accounted for by an historical materialist analysis of transformations underway within contemporary capitalism towards more flexible forms of accumulation (Smart 1992).

OLD TROUBLES

At times it might seem as though the current disputation over modernity and postmodernity is a late twentieth-century replay of the quarrel between the ancients and the moderns (Bock 1979; Calinescu 1977). Certainly there is a sense in which the veneration of things modern has been placed in question, if not brought to a close, by the idea of a postmodern condition of knowledge. However, the comparison is ultimately misleading, because it is assumptions about progress and developments in knowledge and culture that provided the basis of the argument that modernity is a distinctive and superior period in the history of humanity, that are called into question or subjected to doubt by the idea of postmodernity. In other words postmodernity can make no credible claim to be a superior stage of human history.

Another sense in which an allusion appears to be made to the possibility that history is repeating itself occurs when reference is made to the significance of the approaching *fin de siècle* in diagnoses of current conditions as postmodern. We are reminded that at the end of the nineteenth century there was an 'anxious and despairing mood' (Jay 1988) and that the earlier *'fin de siècle* spirit and the current wave of postmodern culture share a common rhetoric of rebellion against the Enlightenment narrative' (Mestrovic 1991). In other words there are some interesting parallels to be drawn between the late nineteenth century and our own time. However, there are also significant differences to be noted between the respective periods, not least of all concerning the prospects for realising socialism, conceived as a higher, progressive form of life which provides the necessary conditions for human potential to be expressed, developed and fulfilled. The revolutionary events of 1989 in Eastern Europe and the overthrowing of the 1991 coup in the Soviet Union have lent weight to the observation that 'the entire progressivist discourse in which certain classes or countries were understood as the cutting edge of a world-historical movement', the related idea of an aesthetic and/or political avant-garde, and the associated notion of redemption, the 'concept of a redeemed social being' (Jay 1988: 11–12) are to be regarded with great suspicion. It is now necessary to go beyond the traditional socialist project by recognising that all social struggles are partial struggles and that their objectives are specific emancipations rather than the 'global emancipation of humanity'; the plurality of struggles is in turn correlated with a proliferation of subject positions which themselves are articulated in complex ways; and finally that it is more appropriate to talk of 'local' socialisms, for 'socialist demands can only be articulated to other democratic demands . . . and these will vary from country to country' (Laclau 1990: 225). So, whilst there might be significant continuities between present times and the end of the nineteenth century, a possibility to which I have already drawn attention, there are clearly important differences to which we have a responsibility to attend.

A more ambitious variant on the *fin de siècle* (post)modern parallels thesis is provided by Umberto Eco (1987) who compares the social, economic, political and cultural configuration, and associated concerns, prominent at the end of the first millennium in Europe with their end-of-second-millennium 'equivalents'. An analytic return to the transformations associated with the era in which 'modern Western man came to maturity' is portrayed by Eco as helpful for understanding 'what is happening in our own day' (1987: 75). It is not a matter of identifying direct parallels across a thousand-year span, but rather of noting that a number of 'medieval' preoccupations appear, once again, to have a con-temporary resonance, that our age may in a number of significant respects be described as 'neomedieval'. The reasons advanced by Eco in support of this contention include a number of brief observations on the current renewal of interest in the Middle Ages, exemplified by fictions of various kinds, the respects in which 'the Western legacy, and all the problems of the Western world emerged in the Middle Ages' (1987: 64), and finally aspects of present conditions that may be argued to be 'neomedieval'.

It would be wrong to infer that a preoccupation with the Middle Ages is a feature peculiar to our own time. On the contrary it is apparent that ever since the onset of the modern era people have made attempts to uncover their roots in some version of the Middle Ages. Having identified this feature of the modern era Eco asks 'what distinguishes this permanent dis-covery of the Middle Ages from the equally permanent return to the classical heritage?' (1987: 67). The answer given is that our distant reconstructions of classical antiquity only furnish us with 'ideal models', whereas our lives continue to be lived with(in), or in the shadows of, the patched-up remains of medieval institutions (e.g. bank, church, state, university). The aspects of social and political conditions that lead Eco to consider our age to be neomedieval include the following.

First the dismantling or breaking up of a great peace or order which in turn creates a power vacuum and precipitates economic crisis. Eco has in mind what he describes as 'the crisis of the Pax Americana', a crisis which derives from the internal and external shifts and transformations to which the different states of the United States of America have been, and continue to be subject. The sense and reality of economic decline exemplified by the collapse of the automobile industry, the proliferation of imported goods, and the growing foreign ownership of flagship industries and corporations; the reality and fear of crime, violence, drugs and signs of increasing deprivation; and the growing realisation that the 'American way' is being transformed by the growing prominence of constituencies which do not necessarily share the same cultural values, language, traditions, benefits or resources. The radical changes in Eastern Europe since 1989; the reunification of Germany; the end of the Cold War; fundamental social, economic and political transformations in the Soviet Union; moves towards forms of unification, if not federation, within the European Economic Community; and continuing evidence of the rise of Japan, all lend weight to Eco's observations. Notwithstanding the proclaimed success of the American-led United Nations military action in the 1991 Gulf War, the vision of a 'New World Order' has been rapidly distorted by accumulating signs of disorder. The increasing disarray of the Soviet Union has put the question of America's role in the world firmly on the agenda (Chomsky 1991). The possibility that the Soviet Empire came undone, in the final instance because its political and military commitments could not be sustained with an ailing economy, constitutes a potential 'warning for America itself . . . at a time when its own society shows signs of coming apart through drugs, violent crime, racial strife and the failure of education and family structures' (*Observer*, 15 September 1991: 22).

The second aspect identified as symptomatic of the increasingly neomedieval character of our era involves transformations in city life. Eco refers to the 'medievalisation of the city', to the development of microsocieties and 'minorities' neighbourhoods, and an associated increase in tension, conflict and 'fragmentation of the social body' exemplified by increasing concern with security and protection; as well as to the way in which, rather than a decline in population or difficulty of communication and transportation it is excesses of the same that are rendering many cities uninhabitable.

The third and final aspect to be briefly noted here concerns the ' "climate of risk" characteristic of late modernity' (Giddens 1991: 123). In contrast to the early Middle Ages where there was 'a marked technological decline', Eco suggests that we are living within a society that faces the problems (as well as the benefits) of technological development, for example 'gridlocks and malfunctions . . . production of poisonous and carcinogenic foods . . . and useless objects . . . deforestation . . . pollution of water, atmosphere, and vegetation, the extinction of animal species, and so on' (Eco 1987: 78). Such negative consequences of the extension of abstract systems of knowledge and expertise contribute to the risk climate, to the feelings of insecurity identified as symptomatic of our 'neomedievalism'. The implication of which is not that modern social life is reducible solely to the experience of new dangers and threats, but rather that '[h]igh modernity is characterised by widespread skepticism about providential reason, coupled with the recognition that science and technology are double-edged, creating new parameters of risk . . . as well as . . . beneficent possibilities' (Giddens 1991: 27–8).

Does the preoccupation with the Middle Ages exemplify submission to 'postmodern temptation' or does it indicate something else, perhaps that we feel ourselves to be living in an interregnum, or that our age is indeed one of 'permanent transition'? Eco believes it is the latter and that we require new methods of operation and adjustment to cope with the emerging 'culture of constant readjustment' (Eco 1987: 84). In other words we are indeed living in new times, but we continue nevertheless to encounter familiar problems. Critics of the idea of postmodernity and its diverse corollaries place emphasis on the persistence of familiar structures, experiences and problems. In contrast to the identification of a shift from mass-production Keynesian–Fordist forms of economic organisation to post or neo-Fordist flexible forms of accumulation employing various types of CAD/CAM (computer-aided design and manufacturing) systems

(Noble 1984); a relative decline of traditional political movements, parties and affiliations and the rise of different kinds of life politics (Giddens 1991); transformations in culture and communications; and signs of significant differences accumulating around questions of identity, conduct and experience as evidence of 'new times', critics return to notions of modernity, the capitalist mode of production, and various combinations of the two in order to give an account of the conditions we encounter. An appropriate example of such a critical approach to the question of postmodern times is provided by Callinicos who confesses 'I do not believe that we live in "New Times", in a "postindustrial and postmodern age" fundamentally different from the capitalist mode of production globally dominant for the past two centuries' (1989: 4). Well, we are all entitled to our beliefs perhaps. And the question of new times is certainly one we should approach with a healthy degree of scepticism. But there seems to be a misunderstanding, or worse, an intentional misrepresentation present in this confession and the ensuing discussion, namely that the adoption of notions of new times, postindustrialism, and postmodern conditions in analysis needs must lead to the exclusion of any consideration of the capitalist mode of production and its relevance for understanding significant aspects of contemporary conditions.

The positions critically addressed by Callinicos are occupied by Marxist analysts who employ a notion of 'new times' in a positive rather than a negative sense, and Lyotard who opens one of his contributions on contemporary conditions with the 'working hypothesis . . . that the status of knowledge is altered as societies enter *what is known* as the postindustrial age and cultures enter *what is known* as the postmodern age' (1986: 3, emphasis added). In neither case is a concept of the postmodern or postmodernity employed simply in contradistinction to, or in a periodising sense as displacing, a notion of the modern or modernity. Moreover, both the Marxist analyses of new times alluded to by Callinicos and Lyotard's reflections on postmodern conditions explicitly affirm the continuing relevance and significance of an analysis of capitalism for an understanding of our era. Modern and postmodern conditions, modernity and postmodernity, are conceived to be closely related, and the implied transformations and differences are recognised as closely articulated with a persisting, developing capitalist mode of production. In the case of the respective works of Hebdige (1988, 1989) on

new times, postmodern cultural forms, and contemporary capitalist production of commodities, services and consumers; Soja
(1989) on the spatial implications of post-Fordist capitalist processes of 'postmodernisation'; and Harvey (1989) on the complex
interpenetration within 'capitalist society as a whole' of 'fordist
modernity' and 'flexible postmodernity', the question of the
forms of articulation between the respective elements is central.
Typically, critical Marxist responses to concepts of new times
and postmodernity have sought to demonstrate that they 'grossly
exaggerate the extent of the changes involved' (Callinicos 1989:
135), and/or to reveal the significant (unacknowledged) instance
of determination attributable to the continuing development of
the capitalist mode of production. A more controversial and far
from typical response has been to acknowledge the existence of
postmodern conditions and then proceed to explore the wide-
ranging and, in many respects, radical epistemological-analytical
and political consequences for Marxism. Although there are vestiges of such a response in Hebdige's call for a 'marxism without
guarantees' (1988: 207) and Soja's identification of the need for
a 'postmodern deconstruction and reconstitution' (1989: 64) of
Marxism, it is the works of Laclau and Mouffe that are most
closely associated with a radical exploration of the implications
of postmodern conditions for Marxism (Smart 1992).

A few brief references in *Hegemony and Socialist Strategy*
(1985) to a 'post-Marxist terrain' seem to have set the agenda for
readings by Marxist critics. Interpreted as placing itself 'beyond
Marxism', a seemingly self-evident heresy, Laclau and Mouffe's
work is described as not 'theoretically worthwhile in any substantive respect' and as a 'product of the very advanced stage of an
intellectual malady' (Geras 1987: 42–3). The reason for such a
vigorous critical reaction by Marxists committed to the orthodox
line is that *Hegemony and Socialist Strategy* systematically takes
issue with many of the long-cherished assumptions of Marxism.
The explanation given by Laclau and Mouffe for critically exploring the Marxist tradition once again is that the ' "evident truths"
of the past . . . have been seriously challenged by an avalanche
of historical mutations which have riven the ground on which
those truths were constituted' (1985: 1). Another alternative
would perhaps be to ignore the historical mutations, the awkward
and paradoxical events, or insist they fit into our longstanding
'sacred' categories. Laclau and Mouffe evidently consider that
a long history of social and political 'anomalies', the 'radical

questioning of the logic of foundations', and the signs in the streets of new non-class forms of struggle and conflict ('the rise of the new feminism, the protest movements of ethnic, national and sexual minorities, the anti-institutional ecology struggles . . . the anti-nuclear movement, the atypical forms of social struggle in countries on the capitalist periphery' (1985: 1) warrant more than yet another repetition of familiar analytic and political platitudes.

The tenets of Marxism challenged by Laclau and Mouffe include:

(i) the idea that class as a structural analytic category constitutes the primary determinant of identity; social conduct and relationships; political affinities, and associated forms of expression;

(ii) the primacy accorded to economic conditions as explanatory variables;

(iii) the relative marginalisation of non-economic factors and variables;

(iv) the viability of the premises of materialist method outlined in the *German Ideology* and reconceived in *The 1859 Preface* in the form of what has come to be known as the base and superstructure metaphor (Hall 1977);

(v) the attribution of *objective* interests and a privileged historical role to an *analytically* constructed *social* constituency, the working class;

(vi) socialism as the unquestioned objective or emancipatory end of politics; and

(vii) the possibility of a totalising explanatory framework which renders social and historical development intelligible (Geras 1987: 43–4).

In response Marxist critics have asked what remains? What kind of Marxism, if any, can be reconstituted from the ruins left by Laclau and Mouffe's challenge? But such questions already betray the defensive strategy to which many Marxists have been driven by the limitations intrinsic to their paradigm. The tenets of Marxism noted above have always been problematic, always been in contention both within and without the Marxist tradition. To that extent nothing very much has changed, and Laclau and Mouffe are perfectly justified in situating their project within the long 'history of marxism [which] has met with several such nodal moments of ambiguity and discursive proliferation' (Laclau 1988: 74). The implied idea of a 'crisis of Marxism' is of course by no means new; it has been virtually synonymous with Marxism itself (Jay 1988). What perhaps is different now is that the radically reflexive processes of questioning which developed in tandem with modern forms of life extend to and encompass modernity itself. As Giddens comments, we increasingly find ourselves 'left with questions where once there appeared to be answers and . . . it is not only philosophers who realise this. A general awareness of the phenomenon filters into anxieties which press in on everyone' (1990: 49). Certainly Laclau and Mouffe's thesis has challenged the central assumptions and called into question the answers generated within the Marxist paradigm, and in consequence it has provoked a highly charged critical response.

Would it have made a difference if the authors had referred from the outset to the prospects and possibilities for a postmodern Marxism, rather than describe their contribution as a 'post-Marxist' project? If they had explicitly located themselves, as subsequently they have sought to do, 'squarely within the discussion around postmodernity from the point of view of marxism' (Laclau 1988: 78) some of the misunderstandings which have arisen might well have been avoided. However, in the final instance, and in these matters it always seems to arrive, the qualification that ' "postmarxism" is not an "ex-marxism" ' (Laclau 1988: 77) is not enough for critics who want nothing less than an unqualified endorsement of Marxist analysis and politics. The combination of Marxism with postmodern ideas is frequently regarded as 'peculiar or paradoxical'. Indeed if the intellectual and/or political response to the idea of postmodernity appears to fall short of open disavowal it is likely that the author will be considered to have 'gone off the deep end and become a "post-Marxist" (which is to say a renegade and a turncoat)' (Jameson 1989: 32). So much for the prospects of a fraternal exchange of ideas.

One of the leading figures in the debate over postmodern conditions who does fit the description 'ex' or 'post' Marxist is Lyotard. From the early 1950s to 1964 Lyotard was a member of the 'critical Marxist', 'quasi-Trotskyist' group *Socialisme ou Barbarie* (Veerman 1988; Callinicos 1989) and then, very briefly, another group, *Pouvoir ouvrier*. From the mid-1960s it is evident that Lyotard's work became further and further removed from the established analytic assumptions and political strategies of

Marxism. A sequence of events in Europe, 'Berlin 1953, Budapest 1956, Czechoslovakia 1968, [and] Poland 1980', have raised serious doubts about 'the doctrine of historical materialism' (Lyotard 1988a: 179). In each case workers rose up against the Communist Party and in each instance the challenge *appeared* to have been extinguished. With the benefit of hindsight these complex historical moments may be regarded as portents of things to come, early signs of the momentous transformations which occurred in Eastern Europe during the late 1980s. Indeed the significance of these earlier events has been surpassed by the 1989 'revolutions' in Eastern Europe and the 1991 popular and successful opposition to the attempted Communist Party coup in the Soviet Union. The signs in the streets of Moscow, Berlin, Prague, Budapest, and Warsaw are now a little different. However, in what respects, if at all, the events identified constitute a wholesale refutation of historical materialism remains a contentious matter (Callinicos 1991).

The events briefly noted above have contributed to, and to an extent exemplify, the process of erosion of legitimacy and credibility to which Marxism as a 'grand narrative' of emancipation has become subject. In so far as Lyotard's work in general, and the essay *The Postmodern Condition: A Report on Knowledge* (1986) in particular, addresses developing problems of analytic credibility and political legitimacy, the more recent difficulties to which Marxist analysis and politics have become vulnerable appear to have been anticipated. Predictably such 'anticipations' have not been well received and as tends to be the case in these matters it is the messenger who is taken to task. And Lyotard, in one respect at least, presents a relatively soft target for those who recognise only two positions on the political spectrum. The strategy employed to counter Lyotard's critical reflections on analysis and politics has been to argue that leaving the critical Marxism of *Socialisme ou Barbarie* behind effectively signifies a move to the right. The clear implication being that the subsequent attention drawn by Lyotard to forms of politics that are manifestly not working, the doubts articulated about prospects for a singular, totalising emancipatory politics, as well as the necessary questions raised about what might be done, and what forms of resistance might be possible in present conditions, constitute betrayals, signs of reaction, or evidence of subscription to a form of neoconservativism.

Lyotard is not, of course, alone in asking questions and raising doubts about the 'grand narrative' of emancipatory politics. Other analysts interested in trying to understand the revolutionary transformations of our time have suggested that developments in the course of the twentieth century make 'any notion of an emancipatory politics deeply problematic' (Sayer 1991: 154) and that 'the socialist project . . . presented as the global emancipation of humanity . . . has today gone into crisis' (Laclau 1990: 225). Describing those analysts who attempt something more than a reduction of the complexities of the present to an abstract model derived from the past as revisionists, reactionaries or neoconservatives does not serve to enhance understanding; on the contrary it exemplifies yet another sign of the increasing reversion to fundamentalisms of one kind or another, what has been described as the dark side of postmodernity (Sacks 1991). Furthermore, it is the shaky foundations on which such fundamental analytical and political 'certitudes' have been predicated that are most disturbed by Lyotard's work. As with Foucault's genealogical approach to social analysis (Smart 1985, 1986), Lyotard casts doubt on the universalising pretensions of modern intellectual practice by arguing that,

> it is probable now and for the foreseeable future [that] we, as philosophers, as much as we may be concerned by politics (and inevitably we are so concerned), are no longer in a position to say publicly: 'Here is what you must do' . . . This is not to say that there are no longer any intellectuals, but that today's intellectuals, philosophers in so far as they are concerned by politics and by questions of community, are no longer able to take up obvious and pellucid positions: they cannot speak in the name of an 'unquestionable' universality.
>
> (1988b: 301)

Implied here is one of the central themes in the debate over modern and postmodern conditions, notably that we may be witnessing a relative shift of emphasis from legislative to interpretive forms of intellectual inquiry (Bauman 1987).

It would be relatively easy in the midst of all the controversial matters briefly identified above to lose sight of the reason for addressing Lyotard's work in this context. My concern is to show that notwithstanding his identification of postmodern conditions there is a clear recognition of the continuing relevance of aspects of Marxist analysis for an understanding of ongoing transformations in the capitalist mode of production. In brief, for Lyotard 'Marxism has not come to an end' (1988a: 171); the question is '[h]ow must we read Marx today?' (1989: 23). The answer Lyotard provides is that we must read Marx critically. The problem is that 'Marxism is one of the versions of the Enlightenment' and the intellectual politics at the centre of Marxism rests on the imagined universality of the figure of the proletariat. As Gorz (1982), Laclau (1990) and others have demonstrated convincingly '[w]hat we don't have is that universalisation' (Lyotard 1989: 26). But if Lyotard casts doubt on the adequacy and appropriateness of the politics of Marxism, the value and relevance of Marxist analysis for generating an understanding of the continuing development of capitalism remains. As Lyotard explains,

> the complexification due to new technologies in both everyday life and the work-process (and working conditions) makes this traditional province of Marxism more and more important and serious. It is obvious for example that the level of unemployment foreseen by Marx – and created not by the crisis of capitalism but by the development of capitalism – is today a reality. And we have no solution to that. I think this will be the main problem for the next century because it's impossible to consider a mankind in which only one person in ten is working. It's perfectly possible to elaborate this problem in Marxist terms.
>
> (1989: 21)

However, 'main problem' does not mean the whole problem, the total picture, or the complete story. It is clear that for Lyotard a Marxist analysis of the contemporary development of capitalism only tells us some things, albeit potentially important and valuable things, about the complex and problematic conditions we now encounter. The implication is that something more than a reflex rejection of the idea of postmodern conditions and parallel re-affirmation of the assumed unity, coherence and correctness of a given Marxist line, and something less than a wholesale abandonment of Marxism is required. Perhaps a willingness, in the light of 'postmodern preoccupations' (Sayer 1991: 5, 57) to reconsider Marxism as simply one point of reference in a reconstructed critical tradition (Smart 1992). What other options are there? As Laclau cautions,

If a tradition ceases to be the cultural terrain where creativity and the inscription of new problems take place, and becomes instead a hindrance to that creativity and that inscription, it will gradually and silently be abandoned. Because any tradition may die. In that sense Marxism's destiny as an intellectual tradition is clear: it will either be inscribed as a historical, partial and limited moment within a wider historical line, that of the radical tradition of the West, or it will be taken over by the boy scouts of the small Trotskyist sects who will continue to repeat a totally obsolete language – and thus nobody will remember Marxism in twenty years' time.

(1990: 179)

(POST)MODERNITY

The idea of postmodernity indicates a modification or change in the way(s) in which we experience and relate to modern thought, modern conditions and modern forms of life, in short to modernity. However, in so far as modernity is itself continually in a state of flux, perpetually in motion, or processual in character the idea of a condition of postmodernity must, in turn, be situated in relation to developments and transformations in sociality, culture and communications, technological innovation and economic production, and political life. I have discussed a number of these aspects of transformation and their implications in *Modern Conditions, Postmodern Controversies* (Smart 1992). In the following chapters I concentrate on the relational sense of postmodernity noted above and consider in particular its contribution to our understanding of contemporary sociology and the analysis of social life; the characteristics of modernity and its consequences; contemporary political conditions and opportunities; the persistence or regeneration of religious belief; and finally the complex and confusing forms of articulation between, on the one hand, global processes and associated interdependencies and on the other hand the inescapabilities and particularities of local forms and identities.

2
The disorder of things

The relatively sudden and unanticipated end of the Cold War that chilled Europe for over forty years appears to be turning into an ever more complicated peace. Moreover, one of the seemingly most liberal and peaceful of the former 'societies of actually existing socialism', Yugoslavia, has subsequently provided the setting for an increasingly complicated war, the first 'hot' war since 1945 in Europe. Meanwhile, in an America buoyed up by both the 'successful' outcome of the Gulf War and the collapse of the 'Evil Empire' there is increasing concern about the troubles at home, including in extreme cases expression of fears about the possibility of civil war. The diminishing threat of global apocalypse has seemingly been replaced by the growing reality of 'local' catastrophe. Evidence of increasing racial and ethnic conflict has been taken as a sign that the assimilatory model of the 'melting pot' is no longer appropriate. The aspiration now is not assimilation but 'integration through diversity' which means according legitimacy and value to ethnic and religious identities, communities and differences 'so long as they are ultimately subordinated to the overarching political community and its complex of myths, memories and symbols' (Smith

1990: 173). The growing social problems and conflicts threatening community life in America demonstrate that if integration through diversity is the aspiration, fragmentation, aggression and disintegration is the more familiar reality. Crimes of violence appear to be rising rapidly. In 1991 the projection was for 24,000 homicides. Of every 1000 Americans, 11 were expected to be victims of violent crime. In education 25 per cent of all High School students were expected to fail to graduate. And the economic portents appeared equally gloomy. The budget deficit was projected to be $350 billion and over 33 million Americans were considered to face the prospect of living below the poverty line. Moreover, once dominated by domestic capital, the economy 'is now increasingly influenced by transnationally orchestrated foreign investment, especially from Britain, Canada, Germany, the Netherlands, and Japan' (Rouse 1991: 16). Do such developments constitute signs of 'the eclipse of America' (Wark 1990: 20), do they suggest that as we move rapidly from 'the territorial-military-political age into an economic-financial-technological age . . . [the] United States due to its economic, budgetary and societal shortcomings, is bound to lose political and, ultimately, also military clout' (Sommer 1991: 10)?

One possible implication of these developments is perhaps the emergence of a 'new world order', but not quite the order American President George Bush seemed to have in mind when he articulated his 1990 vision of a post-Cold War world. The idea and implied possibility of an orderly world is a familiar feature of modernity as an accomplished form of social life, a form of life bound up with the growth of Enlightenment. However, it is clear that the emerging 'new order' is paralleled by manifestations of extensive and intensive forms of disorder. Not for the first time the promise of modernity to cultivate orderliness in the world simultaneously precipitates an awareness of forms of disorder, not so much as symptoms of failure, incompletion or lack of realisation, but rather as necessary corollaries of the pursuit of order itself.

The idea of order as a task, as a practice, as a condition to be reflected upon, preserved and nurtured is intrinsic to modernity. The modern quest for order constitutes 'the least possible among the impossible and the least disposable among the indispensable; indeed [it is] the archetype for all other tasks, [the] one that renders all other tasks mere metaphors of itself' (Bauman 1991a: 4). Order and disorder are inextricably connected, they are simultaneously constituted and spiral in a double-helix-like fashion around the axis of modernity. Hence the perpetual preoccupation with the elimination or reduction of forms of disorder through the engineering and management of orderliness in modern forms of life. A preoccupation which is regenerated and reconstituted through the realisation that ordering interventions seem to promote other disorders, to precipitate effects or 'unintended consequences' of disorder.

The social sciences have played a prominent part in the development of the intellectual and political ordering of modernity. As Giddens remarks,

> The practical impact of social sciences is both profound and inescapable. Modern societies, together with the organisations that compose and straddle them, are like learning machines, imbibing information in order to regularise their mastery of themselves. Because of the perversity of unintended consequences, and the very contingency of social change, we may presume that such mastery will always be less than complete. Yet upon our capabilities for social learning, in the world that is the legacy of modernity, we predicate our future. Only societies reflexively capable of modifying their institutions in the face of accelerated social change will be able to confront the future with any confidence. Sociology is the prime medium of such reflexivity.
>
> (1987: 21)

Sociology as a 'medium' is a corollary of modernity, a discursive practice which both contributes to and participates in the quest for order, yet simultaneously reflects critically upon the consequences, the problems and the difficulties. And in what might be described as its tentative engagement with the idea of 'postmodernity' sociology reflects critically upon modernity itself.

SOCIOLOGY AND MODERNITY

The emergence and development of sociology as a distinctive form of inquiry is generally recognised to be synonymous with the advent of modernity (cf. Bierstedt 1979; Bock 1979). The formation of sociology – the delineation of a distinctive field of inquiry, constitution of subject matter, and development of appropriate methodology – has had as its objective an analytic ordering of social phenomena and an associated provision of social technologies directed towards a government of social life and the achievement of a degree of rational control over social development. It is on these broad terms and assumptions that sociology has taken its place within the modern order of things, within the 'project of modernity'.

On a number of levels and in a variety of different discourses the feasibility, validity, relevance and value of modern sociology has begun to be questioned, perhaps most explicitly in analyses which have identified possible limits to the project of modernity and an increasing disorder of things modern arising from what has been termed the development of 'postmodernism' or advent of 'postmodernity' (cf. Featherstone 1988; Bauman 1988a, 1988b, 1990a, 1991b). However, expression of concern over the condition of modern sociology is not confined to contemporary reflections on 'postmodernity'. An interest in the state and possible fate of the discipline is longer-standing and certainly predates current conceptual and theoretical preoccupations. Indeed it might be argued that in some respects past reflections on the discipline anticipate themes and issues which have been subsequently articulated in terms of the question of the relationship of sociology and postmodernity (cf. Toynbee 1954b: 188–9; Gouldner 1971; Foucault 1973). It is to a consideration of the issues raised in such reflections on the condition of modern sociology that this chapter is directed.

In what now seems like another age Alvin Gouldner warned of an 'impending crisis of sociology' arising from the undermining of the dominant paradigm (functionalism) and the neutralisation of its critical corollary (Marxism). If reactions at the time ranged from curiosity and confusion to disinterest and disagreement it is now possible to recognise that the general thesis advanced by Gouldner was remarkably prescient in its identification of the range of difficulties likely to be encountered by sociology. Whether particular aspects of the crisis were impending, or to a degree already present at the time, is not an issue I intend to pursue here (see Giddens 1987: 255).

In his discussion of the crisis of 'modern' sociology Gouldner identifies three central contradictions developing around the following:

(i) research for the welfare state;

(ii) methodological concern over the question of 'objectivity'; and

(iii) the subject–object dualism.

In respect of the first contradiction it is argued that in order to preserve and nurture the funding relationship there is an increasing tendency for the scope of sociological inquiry to be limited to the 'reformist solutions of the Welfare State'. Such an orientation inevitably exposes sociologists to the 'failures of this state and of the society with whose problems it seeks to cope' (1971: 439). Whilst such sociological work is likely to enhance awareness of and in turn increase sensitivity to human anguish and difficulty, there exists in addition a substantial counter-pressure, namely a professional vested interest in both the persistence of social problems and the continuing availability of funds for their study. As Gouldner cryptically comments, 'careers depend on it'. Or to be more precise, the '[m]odern state and modern intellect alike need chaos – if only to go on creating order' (Bauman 1991a: 9). The second contradiction arises from a concern with 'objectivity' in sociological work, a concern which it is suggested leads on the one hand to an accommodation, if not an acceptance of the prevailing order of things, yet on the other hand simultaneously promotes distance from the central values and dominant assumptions of the social order. The call for 'objectivity' either disguises 'capitulation to the status quo' or constitutes a 'protective covering for the critical impulses of the timid' (Gouldner 1971: 439). Either way it is clear from Gouldner's critical comments that the methodological pursuit of 'objectivity' is counterproductive for it serves to conceal the relations of knowledge and power intrinsic to sociological research. The final contradiction identified is one which might be regarded as central to if not constitutive of the discipline (cf. Berger and Luckmann 1975; Dawe 1979; Giddens 1979). In Gouldner's terms it is a contradiction between the *'focal* assumption that society makes man' and the *'tacit* assumption that man makes society' (1971: 440). The suggestion is that whilst an emphasis upon the social and cultural constitution of forms of human subjectivity may have been liberatory in a context where biologistic and supernatural explanations predominated, in a 'secularized and bureaucratic society such as our own' the emphasis placed on social and cultural factors effectively serves to reinforce and normalise the prevailing conditions and forces to which human beings are subject. The conclusion to which Gouldner is drawn is the articulation of a 'liberative' and 'reflexive' sociology which shifts the emphasis to the constitutive character of human action and conduct. It is a conclusion which may now be read as anticipating the contemporary preoccupation with the ambiguous figure of 'the subject' (Heller 1990a).

Whether Gouldner is successful in delivering an alternative form of sociology, a 'radical or neo-sociology', from what is conceived to be an ideologically conservative academic sociology is not something I intend to pursue here. It is perhaps worth adding that such a goal seems to have remained firmly on the sociological agenda (cf. Bauman 1988a). What I want to draw attention to is the presence in Gouldner's modernist project of a number of problems and concerns which have subsequently been re-articulated in deliberations on 'postmodernity' and sociology. For example, the 'funding tie' to the state has indeed become a matter of concern, but not only for the compromises it might make necessary. Part of the existing crisis derives from a dramatic reduction in the funding of sociological work by the state and the absence of alternative compensating sources. Paraphrasing Gouldner it might be argued that through its patronage of social science research the state has been inadvertently exposed to the limits of sociological inquiry, the limitations of associated forms of social engineering, and the intractable complexity of social processes. Accumulating doubts about the fiscal, political and social consequences of social engineering and the corollary, a more coordinated administration or management of social life, have led the state to reconsider, if not reduce its 'investment' in social research in general and sociological work in particular. In respect of methodological concerns plurality and polycentrism have indeed, as Gouldner anticipates, become the order of the day. But the preoccupation with the question of 'objectivity' has been effectively displaced by the development of new forms of theory and methodology, the promotion of various forms of commitment and critique, and the increasing prominence accorded to the idea that there is a 'crisis of the foundations' of knowledge (Lyotard 1986, 1988b). Finally, if the subject–object dualism has continued to be a central issue within sociology, the terms of the debate have been radically revised and transformed (cf. Giddens 1979, 1982). The proposal outlined by Gouldner for a 'reflexive' sociology represents an attempt to counterbalance the emphasis placed upon the structural determination of forms of human subjectivity and conduct within sociology. But it leaves unresolved the contradictions associated with the subject–object dualism. Whether these have been resolved or simply recast by Giddens's 'structuration theory' continues to be a matter of debate (cf. Dallmayr 1982).

The forms of intellectual disorder addressed by Gouldner have not diminished. On the contrary there has been a subsequent proliferation of new forms of theory and analysis and the contradictions identified have persisted, if not become more acute. The accumulation of different forms of theory and method, the persistence of associated differences in analytic focus and conceptualisation of subject matter, and related unresolved disputes over questions of epistemology and ontology exemplify the diversity and disagreement which is a prominent feature of contemporary sociology. Whether the 'proliferation of theoretical traditions' will continue to be a significant feature of sociology remains at present an open question (cf. Giddens 1987). What is more certain is that the process of questioning to which contemporary sociology has become increasingly subject is closely articulated with transformations in, or possibly of, modernity itself. Transformations which may indicate the emergence of *post*modern forms, or the advent of a condition of postmodernity.

If sociology is indeed bound up with the project of modernity then transformations in or of the latter may have important consequences for the discipline. In their own distinctive ways the analyses to be considered here draw attention to the actual or potential impact of transformations of modernity upon sociology. For example, in an archaeological analysis of the human sciences Foucault (1973) refers to the possibility that the modern *episteme* within which sociology emerged and developed 'is now about to topple'; Baudrillard (1983b) writes enigmatically of the 'end of the social' and with it sociology; Touraine (1984) describes a number of fundamental social and cultural transformations which render the existing 'sociological view of social life' problematic, if not increasingly irrelevant; Giddens (1987) outlines a number of theses for the future development of sociology which are necessary for an adequate address of a transformed and changing 'modernity'; and finally Bauman (1988a, 1988b, 1990a, 1991b) provides an inventory of topics and tasks to be addressed by a sociology encountering 'postmodernity'.

SOCIOLOGY IN THE ORDER OF THINGS

Sociology occupies a relatively peripheral position in the various studies of the relationships between truth, power and the subject or self conducted by Foucault. However, in so far as several of the analyses developed by Foucault are concerned with the human sciences, notably with their 'rules' of formation, interconnection with relations of power, and constitution of forms of objectivity and subjectivity, it is possible to identify the outline of an analysis of relevance for an understanding of contemporary sociology. Two different forms of analysis of the human sciences appear in Foucault's work. One explores the epistemological configuration within which the human sciences developed, the other the social and political conditions associated with their emergence. Of these the former is of more direct relevance to my discussion here.

Foucault identifies two major discontinuities in the epistemological configuration (*episteme*) of Western culture. The first midway through the seventeenth century initiates the Classical age and the second at the beginning of the nineteenth century marks the emergence of the modern age. It is with the eclipse of Classical thought and the detachment of language from representation, 'when words ceased to intersect with representations and to provide a spontaneous grid for the knowledge of things' (1973: 304), that the human sciences became possible. In the Classical *episteme* there is no place for a conception of 'man as a primary reality with his own density, as the difficult object and sovereign subject of all possible knowledge' (1973: 310). It is only with a redistribution of the *episteme* arising from an interrogation of the source, origin and limits of representation that a 'certain *modern* manner of knowing' begins to emerge, one in which 'man' is constituted as both the subject and object of knowledge within the configuration of modern thought.

It is argued that the modern *episteme* was fragmented from its inception, that it 'exploded in different directions'. Unlike the Classical field of knowledge the modern *episteme* is not perfectly homogeneous or mathematically ordered, 'nor does it unfold, on the basis of a formal purity, a long descending sequence of knowledge progressively more burdened with empiricity' (1973: 346). Rather Foucault conceives of it in spatial terms as a trihedron, the three planes of which comprise *a priori* sciences, pure formal sciences (the mathematical and physical sciences);

a posteriori sciences, empirical sciences (for example those of 'language, life and the production and distribution of wealth'); and philosophical reflection respectively. The human sciences are not considered to be present on or within any of the above planes; their place lies in the ambiguous volume of space constituted by the epistemological arrangement.

It is this 'cloudy distribution . . . that renders the human sciences so difficult to situate, that gives their localization in the epistemological domain its irreducible precariousness, that makes them appear at once perilous and in peril' (Foucault 1973: 347–8). The indeterminate character of the epistemological form of the human sciences leaves a number of methodological and analytical questions and options open. It effectively leaves the human sciences free, or relatively so, to pursue a range of methodological and analytic possibilities, but in addition it means that from the very beginning these sciences are in difficulty, are necessarily precarious and uncertain as sciences by virtue of their location within the modern epistemological configuration. In brief the modern *episteme* constitutes both their condition of existence and the source of their limits and limitations.

As far as sociology is concerned the utilisation of mathematical formalisation, adoption of models and concepts drawn for example from biology, economics, and linguistics, and continual recourse to forms of philosophical analysis and reflection has meant that methodological pluralism, and an associated degree of disorder arising from an incommensurability of many of the paradigms adopted and deployed, has become a persistent feature of the field. Indeed it might be argued that pluralism and polycentrism are constitutive features of the discipline rather than signs of an impending or existing crisis.

If the question of the form of positivity proper to the field of the human sciences has led to a plethora of methodologies, concepts, and constituent models drawn from other domains of knowledge there remains another distinctive feature of the human sciences, namely their relation to representation. Foucault argues that it is the 'representational' categories of function/ norm, conflict/rule, and signification/system that structure the entire field of the human sciences and make it possible for 'man . . . to present himself to a possible knowledge' (1973: 362). Within the human sciences analysis is directed not to 'life, labour and language' in their most transparent state but to representations of human existence in all its diverse forms, through which it is lived, (re-)produced, and experienced. In consequence for the human sciences there is no way around the 'primacy of representation', for it constitutes both their object domain and 'the general pedestal of that form of knowledge, the basis that makes it possible' (1973: 363).

Coextensive with the existence of the human sciences is the perpetual task of attempting to reveal to 'consciousness' the norms, rules, and signifying totalities which constitute its forms and contents. Such a project of demystification is intrinsic to the human sciences. It is an endless project which remains of necessity within the space of representation and continually confronts a residue or remainder of 'something still to be thought'. Paralleling this oscillation 'between the positivity of man taken as object . . . and the radical limits of his being' is another which derives from the relationship between history and the human sciences. History reveals the temporal limits that define both the object and subject of knowledge, it shows that 'everything that has been thought will be thought again by a thought that does not yet exist' (1973: 372). Alongside the human sciences in the dimensions of the unconscious and historicity two critical or counter-sciences of psychoanalysis and ethnology are to be found. Through critical analyses of the unconscious and culture respectively these 'counter-sciences' question the 'region that makes possible knowledge about man in general'.

Psychoanalysis and ethnology 'ceaselessly "unmake" that very man who is creating and re-creating his positivity in the human sciences'(1973: 379) by revealing the concrete figures of finitude ('Desire, Law and Death') and the cultural specificity of the 'Western *ratio*'. Above these two 'counter-sciences' which effectively lead the human sciences back to their epistemological foundation Foucault locates a third 'counter-science', namely linguistics. Linguistics provides both a formal model for the other counter-sciences and in turn directly exposes and contests the field of the human sciences. Through the promise of a 'primary decipherment' which would reveal the deep formal structure(s) of human existence linguistics opens the way for the re-emergence of the question of the being of language. Given the re-emergence of the question of language Foucault speculates that the epistemological configuration which constituted 'man's particular mode of being and the possibility of knowing him empirically' (1973: 385) may be about to disappear.[1]

The burden of Foucault's conclusion is that the questions

raised concerning the modern *episteme* may prepare the way for a future mode of thought, but the form the latter might take is left open in the analysis, save for the qualification that in Western thought 'the being of man and the being of language' have proved to be incompatible. Whether such an analysis warrants the description 'postmodern' (cf. Bell 1976) is a matter of debate. Certainly the reflections in *The Order of Things* 'raise the question of whether Foucault is himself a modern . . . or by having exposed the dialectical illusion of the attempt to think the unthought, has Foucault moved beyond the aims of modern philosophy? Should we think of Foucault as a postmodern philosopher?' (Hoy 1988: 20). If we take Foucault at his word then it appears the analysis remains firmly on the 'threshold of a modernity that we have not yet left behind' (Foucault 1973: xxiv). The speculative conclusion that the modern epistemological configuration, the modern *episteme*, might be about to topple is itself quite explicitly derived from analysis of the 'return' of language exemplified most clearly in literary works informed by a *modernist* sensibility. For example it is in the context of reflections on modernist literature and the works of Artaud and Roussel in particular that Foucault suggests 'man has "come to an end" ', literally brought to his limits by the re-emergence of the being of language which 'gives prominence . . . to the fundamental forms of finitude' (1973: 383). The extent to which such a conclusion constitutes an implicit endorsement of 'structural linguistics' is also open to debate (cf. Dreyfus and Rabinow 1982: 57; Merquior 1985: 55).

When Foucault refers to a possible disarticulation of the modern epistemological configuration the question of the fate of the human sciences, and thereby of sociology, is left in the balance. In the light of contemporary developments and associated reflections on modernity Foucault's analysis may need to be revised. Certainly sociology no longer remains limited to the concepts, models, and methods identified by Foucault. Analysis of the limits and limitations of the modern epistemological configuration, coupled with the parallel development of 'structuralist' and 'post-structuralist' forms of analysis, and increases in inter- and cross-disciplinary work has contributed to the depth and range of concepts and forms of analysis available within sociology. However, as Giddens (1987: 31) has cautioned a proliferation of theories and methodologies by no means resolves the difficulties encountered within sociology. Pluralism and polycentrism along with closer inter-relationships between the various human sciences have increased the level of disorder in the field of sociological inquiry, further blurred the boundaries with related disciplines, and in addition have rendered the object or focus of sociological investigation less distinct. The question of the appropriate object or focus of sociological investigation is a particular matter of concern in the respective works of Touraine, Giddens, and Bauman to be considered later in this chapter.

The analysis presented by Foucault is intended to be inconclusive and open-ended. The objective is to pose questions which 'may well open the way to a future thought' (1973: 386). And to a substantial degree the work has contributed to a partial realisation of that end. Where Foucault proceeds with caution and qualification in considering a possible transformation of the modern *episteme* Baudrillard makes extravagent pronouncements on the media, the masses, the social, and sociology, and practises a form of theorising which as he remarks 'becomes an event in and of itself' (1987: 127).

FORGET SOCIOLOGY? – BAUDRILLARD ON 'THE END OF THE SOCIAL'

A thesis which has attracted considerable attention identifies the development of a condition of postmodernity as the correlate of a combination of complex socioeconomic and technological transformations. These factors in turn are considered to be articulated with the emergence of a 'post-industrial' society (cf. Lyotard 1986: 3; Frankel 1987: 10), or the development of a 'late' or 'disorganised' stage in the capitalist mode of production (cf. Jameson 1984: 63; Lash and Urry 1987: 299; Ryan 1988: 559). A more controversial formulation of these ideas is outlined in a series of essays and polemics by Baudrillard.

Where Foucault identifies two significant discontinuities in the epistemological configuration of Western culture and differentiates between 'Renaissance', 'Classical', and 'modern' forms of thought, Baudrillard outlines three historical 'orders of simulacra' which denote different relationships between simulacra and 'the real' (cf. Baudrillard 1983a; Chen 1987; Kellner 1988). The first order of simulacra is located in the period from the Renaissance to the beginning of the industrial revolution. It is here that Baudrillard locates the emergence of representation, the dissolution of an unquestioned hierarchical ordering of 'natural' signs by the 'counterfeit of the real', by the production of the copy as equivalent to the original, as representing or embodying nature. The first order of simulacra is subject to a 'natural law of value' (Baudrillard 1983a: 83). With the industrial revolution and the prospect of mechanical reproduction a second order of simulacra emerges in which the potential for infinite reproducibility displaces *contrefait*. At this stage 'an "industrial law of value" reigns where technology itself and mechanical reproduction come to constitute a new reality' (Kellner 1988: 244).

Finally with the increasing centrality of communication networks, information technology, the media, and advertising in the post-second world war period, the age in which Bell (1973) identifies the coming of 'post-industrial society', Baudrillard argues that a third order of simulacra develops, one in which there is a radical departure from both the first and second orders, from the 'counterfeit of an original' and the pure series of exact replicas or mass objects respectively (Baudrillard 1983a: 96 ff.). With the third order we encounter Baudrillard's conception of our contemporary condition, a time in which the real world is constituted in and through models and where a 'structural law of value' prevails. The relationship between images, codes, subjects and events is fundamentally transformed. It is no longer possible to appeal to a 'real' referent, for distinctions between representations and objects, ideas and things can no longer be sustained in a world where simulation models predominate. As Baudrillard expresses it, 'one is not the simulacrum and the other the reality: there are only simulacra' and 'what we now have is the disappearance of the referent' (1988a: 21, 50). So, the third order of simulacra is synonymous with models, codes, and digitality. The question of signs, their 'rational destination', reality, reference, 'illusory' effect and meaning, all of that has been erased as everyday life has been invested by models and codes. Describing the new order of simulation Baudrillard comments that '[d]igitality is its metaphysical principle . . . and DNA its prophet. It is in effect in the genetic code that the "genesis of simulacra" today finds its most accomplished form' (1983a: 103–4).

For Baudrillard two particular forces are identified as constitutive of the new 'postmodern' age of simulation, namely the 'media' and the 'masses'. McLuhan's formula of 'the medium is the message' is given a postmodern inflection and becomes 'mass(age) is the message'.[2] It is the 'single process' of the mass and the media which is deemed to precipitate the 'end of the social' and to threaten along with it the discipline of sociology. In Baudrillard's view the extension of electronic mass media, and television in particular, has been associated with a radical transformation of experience, a neutralisation if not a destruction of meaning and signification, an undermining of traditional forms of political strategy, and an end of the 'perspective space of the social'. Rather than simply assuming the existence of 'the social' as obvious or ageless, Baudrillard suggests that it may 'have had only an ephemeral existence, in the narrow gap between the symbolic formations and our "society" where it is dying' (1983b: 67).

The lack of clarity surrounding the idea of 'the social', the enigmatic character of the term 'social relation', and the existence of 'societies without the social' lead Baudrillard to consider the possibility that perhaps the social has never existed. Implied here is the idea that 'things have never functioned socially but symbolically, magically, irrationally' (1983b: 68). From this standpoint there has only ever been simulation of the social and in consequence what might appear currently to constitute a crisis of the social is in fact to be regarded as a 'brutal *de-simulation*', a disintegration of the very idea of the social. A second possibility which is considered is that the social does indeed exist as a ' "rational" control of residues and a rational *production* of residues' (1983b: 73). In this instance it is argued that the social may assume real force, that it commences with those discarded or not integrated by the group (e.g. 'vagrants, lunatics, the sick') and may be extended or promoted through national assistance, social security, and the method of insurance.[3] Here the end of the social is virtually equated with its extension to the whole of society. Reflecting on the latter possibility Baudrillard argues that such an extension does not constitute a positive process for with it the 'whole community becomes residual' and thus subject to the jurisdiction of a social machine which is absorbed into 'administration pure and simple'.

A third possibility is that the social has not always been a 'delusion' or a 'remainder', that it has existed, has meant something, but only in a perspective space provided by second-order simulacra. With the implosion of meaning associated with the development of electronic media of communication and information, perspective space is displaced by that of simulation. In effect 'rational sociality of the contract, dialectical sociality . . .

gives way to the sociality of contact, of the circuit and transistor-ised network' (1983b: 83). With the displacement of perspective space by that of simulation the social is deemed to have come to an end. In consequence there is a problem for the 'representational' discourses of the social sciences in general and sociology in particular, for:

> Sociology can only depict the expansion of the social and its vicissitudes. It survives only on the positive and definitive hypothesis of the social. The reabsorption, the implosion of the social escapes it. The hypothesis of the death of the social is also that of its own death.
>
> (Baudrillard 1983b: 4)

Of the 'single process' of the mass and the media identified as responsible for the end of both the social and sociology I have concentrated so far on one aspect of Baudrillard's argument, on the way in which the development of electronic mass media and the emergence of a third order of simulacra simultaneously precipitate more information yet less meaning and an irresistible 'destruction of the social'. Briefly the media do not produce an extension of the social, or an increase in socialisation, but an 'implosion of the social in the masses'. In turn the masses are considered to 'result from the neutralization and implosion of the social' (1983b: 104).

Description of the mass as without 'attribute, predicate, quality, [and] reference' forces Baudrillard to deploy a series of metaphors in his discussion. The mass is depicted as a spongy referent, a nothingness, a statistical crystal ball, an earth, a highly implosive phenonemon, 'an *in vacuo* aggregation of individual particles, refuse of the social and of media impulses' (1983b: 3), a black hole, and as a 'leitmotif of political demagogy, a soft, sticky, lumpenanalytical notion' (1983b: 4). Baudrillard argues that it is not possible to specify the term, that it has no 'sociological "reality", [and] has nothing to do with any real population, body or specific social aggregate' (1983b: 5). The mass not only has no meaning, it is impossible to make meaning circulate among the masses. The masses oppose and resist the 'ultimatum of meaning', countering it with a refusal of meaning and a 'will to spectacle' that constitutes not an effect of manipulation or mystification but rather an explicit and positive counter-strategy. The masses are described as anonymous, silent, indifferent towards if not beyond recommended ideals and 'enlightened' political practices, and as a category constituted not through self-expression or reflection but through surveys. The existence of the mass or silent majority is 'no longer social, but statistical . . . [its] only mode of appearance is that of the survey' (1983b: 20).

In opposition to the view that the masses may be stimulated and structured by the diffusion of increased information Baudrillard argues that 'information neutralises even further the "social field"; more and more it creates an inert mass impermeable to the classical institutions of the social' (1983b: 25). Beyond comprehension and representation the mass is neither a group-subject nor an object, its existence is that of simulation through a 'meteoric ritual of statistics and surveys' (1983: 31). The silent acceptance and hyperconformity attributed to the masses are described as effective refusals of the social. By virtue of their 'very inertia in the ways of the social . . . the masses go beyond its logic and its limits, and destroy its whole edifice' (1983b: 47).

For Baudrillard the disorder of things modern, associated with the emergence of postmodern conditions, renders sociology redundant. Within the force field constituted by the media and the masses the social dissolves and, supposedly, along with it sociology. Conceiving the social as the primary focus or object of sociological inquiry and dismissing other categories (e.g. 'class', 'power', 'status', 'institution') as merely muddled notions leads Baudrillard to the conclusion that the end of the social is critical for sociology. The description of key sociological concepts as 'muddled notions' can only be regarded as ironic for Baudrillard's texts themselves make a virtue of turbulence and confusion. The equally strange idea that a mysterious agreement has been reached on sociological concepts to preserve a code of analysis, or that 'within sociology you need do no more than conduct quantitative studies, statistical research etc.' (1984: 19) is indicative of Baudrillard's lack of understanding of the diversity of contemporary sociological inquiry. A more pertinent criticism is that in all the references to the implications for sociology of a possible 'end to the social', there is no recognition of the equally, if not more significant sociological concept of society, a term used liberally throughout Baudrillard's writings. For example, when Baudrillard refers to the 'end of the social', the 'disappearance of history', and to our liberation from a 'certain space/ time, a certain horizon where the real is possible' (1988b: 35) a conception of 'society' is continually invoked.[4] Several references are made to the existence of 'societies without the social', 'societies without history', as well as to 'our "society" . . . putting an end to the social' (1983b: 67). However, in each and every instance the concept of 'society' is neither clarified nor elaborated, although it is, as I will endeavour to show below, increasingly in question within sociological discourse itself.

Baudrillard's mischievous proclamation of the demise of sociology is based on an impoverished conception of both the discipline and its subject matter and to that extent it is fundamentally flawed. However, the broader question raised by Baudrillard of the impact of particular processes of transformation on the focus, definition of field, and subject matter of the discipline is important, although far from original, and has received a constructive endorsement within sociology.

ON THE FUTURE OF SOCIOLOGY

The implication present in the analyses outlined above of a number of difficulties confronting sociology is endorsed, albeit in a more muted and sober vein, in the critical yet constructive observations on sociology offered by Touraine, Giddens, and Bauman, each of whom acknowledges the need for a significant re-definition of the field of study.

Modern sociology is considered by Touraine to be in crisis because the social and cultural system with which it has been associated is in the midst of a process of radical transformation. To understand and explain the transformations taking place it is now necessary to generate new intellectual tools and new concepts. The representation of social life which has to date constituted the core of sociology emphasises the idea of modernity and evolution, and tends to equate societal formation with the geopolitical development of nation-states. Touraine believes that on each count the prevailing sociological image of social life has largely lost its explanatory value. The idea of progressive movement or change along an evolutionary path leading societies towards a convergence with hegemonic modern Western forms has been cast aside as more emphasis has begun to be placed on stability rather than transformation, and on the 'rich diversity of so-called traditional cultures' rather than the 'impoverishing homogeneity of modern civilization' (1984: 38). However, the crisis of modernity implied in the above is not all-encompassing, and it certainly does not signify the emergence of a postmodern era or the advent of a postmodern or 'post-historical' society for

Touraine. On the contrary, the very idea of postmodern society is described as 'an extreme sign of the crisis of industrial culture. The new post-industrial culture . . . is both hyper-modern and in rupture with the theory of modernity' (1984: 39). Today it is no longer possible to invoke unproblematically conceptions of social evolutionism or laws of historical development which serve to differentiate and classify societies according to their stage of progress along a trajectory of increasing technological and economic rationalisation. Such processes of rationalisation have become matters of heated debate, their effects closely scrutinised and in so far as they are increasingly associated with social disruption and disorganisation, erosion of cultural diversity, and psychic and ecological damage they are justifiably regarded as problematic.

In addition it is argued by Touraine that a transformation has occurred in the role of the state which effectively reduces its integrative effect. First, there is evidence of increasing opposition to the intervention of the state in social life and to its extension beyond the domains of 'public entrepreneur and participant in international relations'. It is worth adding that its operation as 'public entrepreneur' has in turn been increasingly subject to question. Second, global diffusion of economic activity and trade, and communications media and cultural production, coupled with higher levels of international travel, and a significant increase in supranational political and economic organisations and forums, has precipitated an erosion of the political sovereignty and cultural specificity ascribed to the 'national state', which in turn renders problematic the principle of unity formerly assumed to be constitutive of 'society'. The implication is not, however, that modernised societies are deprived of all unity, rather that social problems and conflicts now achieve a certain unity independently of any external agency or principle (i.e. the state). Touraine initially suggests that in this context,

> the idea of society receives a new meaning: instead of being defined by institutions or a central power, and provided that it can certainly no longer be defined by common values or permanent rules of social organization, society appears to be a field of debates and conflicts whose stake is the social use of the symbolic goods which are massively produced by our post-industrial society.
>
> (Touraine 1984: 40)

In which case, *contra* Baudrillard, we encounter not the 'end of the social' but the end of conceptualising the field of social phenomena simply in terms of the constitutive politico-adminis-trative measures and geopolitical boundaries of the 'national state'. The corollary of which is that it becomes necessary to consider the existence of fields of social phenomena at both an infranational and a supranational level. In short the simple equa-tion of 'social' (level, movement, or problem) with 'national' seems to be no longer viable or sustainable.

Subsequently Touraine has gone further by suggesting that sociology should no longer be conceptualised as the study of society. The concept of society, a fragile and ambiguous 'unity' at the centre of classical sociology, is described as an unstable mixture of 'social modernity and political order' (Touraine 1989: 8), a legacy of the quest to reconcile modernity and its perpetual pursuit of progress with the achievement of a principle of order and unity. The impact of the increasing internationalisation of economic and cultural life on contemporary sociality leads Tou-raine to comment that 'the received image of society' has been undermined, that:

> Social life is no longer perceived as a restricted space for liberty in a universe of necessity but as an indefinite and perhaps infinite space, so that we must abandon not only the conception of the human world as a microcosm within a macrocosm, but also the idea that social life takes place within essential limits which in practice coincide with those of the nation-state and its juridical institutions or educational programs.
>
> (Touraine 1989: 8)

One implication of which is that contemporary sociology needs to be reconstituted around the study of social relations and social change.

A related implication is that the focus of sociological analysis needs to be extended beyond the advanced Western (post) indus-trial capitalist societies, to encompass a diverse range of societies that have generally been ignored, or alternatively subsumed within explanations promoting either a Western materialist evolu-tionism, or a voluntaristic and idealistic culturalism in which the 'analysis of a social system is replaced by a history of the country which is itself subordinated to the idea of a national essence' (Touraine 1984: 43). Sociology can no longer afford to concentrate attention solely on 'modern' industrialised societies to the neglect of 'traditional' societies. However, something more than a simple extension of sociological focus is required. The analytic consequences of recognising that we live less and less 'within a national framework, partly because of the growing international-isation of economy and culture and partly because of the grow-ing divisions within our countries' (Touraine 1989: 14) are con-siderable. But the analytic difficulties now encountered cannot be resolved simply by disposing of the classical sociological notion of 'society'. More is at stake. Just as Western modernisation is no longer a subject of universal acclaim and imitation, so Western reason and its claims to universality are in question, subject to doubt and criticism. As Touraine remarks, the idea 'that the West has overthrown barriers and caused the light of reason to rise over the modern world corresponds more to the opinions of the party of managing elites than to the historical truth' (1989: 29). Under such circumstances the problem which needs to be addressed is the relationship between 'regional' forms of cultural specificity and more 'global' processes of rationalisation and development. It is here, according to Touraine, that a reconsti-tuted sociology must concentrate its attention. In other words the focus of sociology has to be global rather than 'socio-centric, privileging a single type of historical experience' (1989: 30), and directed towards an understanding of processes of movement or change and their consequences, in particular for the realisation of democratic forms of social and political life.

In the course of a more systematic and rigorous address of the question of the future of sociology Giddens endorses many of the changes identified as necessary by Touraine but develops the discussion beyond a singular concern with the substantive focus of sociological inquiry to encompass questions of method-ology and the practical implications of sociological work. Giddens notes that changes in technology ('the impact of the computer and robotics'), the structure of Western economies (the growth of 'services' and Eastward transfer of industrial production), and the development of an 'increasingly integrated global division of labour' (1987: 16), together with evidence of political changes in Western democracies (e.g. increasing political disaffection, the rise of 'new' movements, and realignments in political support), and comparable transformations in the political structures, cul-tures, and economies of non-Western societies, make an overhaul of sociological theories and concepts long overdue. But if it is time to 'shed the residue of nineteenth and early twentieth-century social thought' (1987: 26) it is not because the project of modernity has been lost in the turbulence produced by the fluctuating currents of 'postmodernity'. On the contrary, Giddens argues that the developments considered to be an embodiment of postmodernity are symptoms of the global extension and diffusion of modernity and associated disintegration or 'dissolution of the traditional world'. In short sociology still remains bound up with modernity; however, the latter is not reduced simply to the 'expansion of *capitalism*' or the 'spread of *industrialism*', but rather it includes at least three other parameters, namely the development of administrative and governmental technologies, military power, and a 'partially autonomous' cultural dimension (1987: 26–9).

In addition to recommending changes in the substantive focus of sociological inquiry, in particular the need to come to terms with the increasingly global character of aspects of social life and the possible emergence of a world system, Giddens advances a number of additional theses on the future of sociology which return us to some of the concerns articulated in diverse ways by Gouldner, Foucault, and Baudrillard. Giddens accepts that there has been a degree of disorder within sociological inquiry following the disintegration of the 'orthodox consensus' but questions the necessity of a wide diversity of methodologies. If there has been a disarticulation of the epistemological configuration within which sociology has been located and an erosion of its prevailing paradigm, the ensuing proliferation of theoretical traditions need not in Giddens's view persist. On the other hand there can be no prospect of a unified theoretical framework for sociology. What is anticipated is a reduction in the degree of diversity through the establishment of a number of agreed parameters within which (normal) sociological analysis will be located and will continue to produce a variety of contested interpretations of social life. The implication would appear to be that a circumscribed methodological pluralism will remain an intrinsic feature of the field of inquiry.[5]

From the problem of an excess of diversity at an intra-disciplinary level Giddens turns to the question of inter-disciplinary relations and emphasises the importance of recognising that the conventional boundaries between sociology and anthropology, and sociology and history have been shifting, and that distinctions between sociology, economics, and political science (and we might add geography and philosophy) need to be reviewed.[6] This is an old problem, one that has been present from the moment attempts were first made to constitute sociology as a distinctive discipline with its own field of inquiry. Its re-emergence as a significant issue arises from an increase in inter-disciplinary work and the constitution of 'cross-disciplinary' fields of inquiry (e.g. cultural studies, feminist studies, social policy analysis and research). It also reflects another concern addressed by Giddens, namely the need to re-think the object of sociological analysis.

In contrast to Baudrillard's confinement of sociology to the figure of the social the reflections on the dominant object of sociological analysis offered by Giddens parallel those of Touraine and concern the need to redefine 'society'. Giddens observes that the conception of 'society' which has predominated within sociological analysis has been assumed to be equivalent to the territorial or geopolitical formation of the modern nation-state. This has meant that both the nation-state, and its articulation with the idea of society, have remained largely untheorised in sociology.[7] The implicit equation of 'societies' with modern nation-states has contributed to the neglect in sociological analysis of 'pre-modern oral cultures and agrarian states', as Giddens describes them, or 'societies without the social' in Baudrillard's terms. In addition the lack of analysis of the articulation of nation-states and societies has left sociology ill equipped to consider the inter-relationship and effect of transformations located at each level.

As Giddens observes, 'sociologists have failed to come to terms conceptually with fundamental factors which make the societies they analyze "societies" at all' (1987: 33). The impact of geopolitical factors and global processes on 'social organisation' and the extension of 'social relations' beyond the borders of nation-states suggests that the concept 'society' is likely to remain a highly ambiguous term. This does not represent a plea for the reconstitution of a conception of society as a single inter-connected whole; on that score I share the concern expressed by Hirst and Woolley that 'it is not necessary in order to analyse the effectiveness of social relations to maintain that they form one interconnected whole' (1982: 24). It is merely to re-affirm the necessity of sorting out the present confusion (and conflation) of references to society, social system, social organisation, social life, and network of social relations.[8]

POSTMODERNITY AND SOCIOLOGY: PROBLEMS AND POSSIBILITIES

There is now an increasing recognition that complex contemporary socioeconomic, cultural, political, and technological transformations, and parallel aesthetic, intellectual, and epistemological developments do not merely represent a temporary interruption of longer-term developmental patterns but indicate the emergence of distinctively different forms. Whether such changes are conceptualised in terms of the development of a late, disorganised, consumer, industrial capitalism bearing a hypermodern cultural formation, or the emergence of a post-industrial society embodying a 'postmodern' sensibility there appears to be a considerable degree of concordance that things are no longer quite as they might once have seemed to be.

On one side there are self-confessed non-sociologists like Foucault and Baudrillard whose respective analyses suggest that the conditions of existence of the social and human sciences are precarious. In particular Baudrillard's 'postmodern' conjectures concerning: the existence of an abyss of meaning; the end not only of the social but also the real as referential; and 'theory as simulation', appear to write off the very possibility (or point) of doing sociology. On the other, sociologists like Touraine and Giddens acknowledge the presence of fundamental problems confronting the discipline, but in turn imply that in one form or another it was ever so, and that the current condition of sociology, if critical, is far from terminal. But then both Touraine and Giddens appear to assume the persistence of modernity, the presence of change within, by implication, fixed parameters or limits, and in consequence the question of postmodernity is rendered peripheral, if it is not actually dismissed in their respective analyses. It is through the works of Bauman that the question of postmodernity has been placed firmly on the sociological agenda.

In delineating a distinctive place for a concept of postmodernity in sociology Bauman employs the term to refer to an experience, a world-view, and a fully fledged social system. Briefly it is argued that the concept of postmodernity captures and articulates a novel experience, one it might be noted unanticipated by the seers of post-industrial society who assume an increase in the status and standing of intellectual work. Bauman argues that on three counts the intellectuals' experience of postmodernity has been one of 'anxiety, out-of-placeness, [and] loss of direction'. First, intellectuals today encounter the impossibility of providing an 'authoritative solution to the questions of cognitive truth, moral judgement, and aesthetic taste' (1988a: 219); an erosion of their traditional legitimatory function by more economic and efficient mechanisms of 'seduction and repression'; and finally displacement from a (potential) position of influence and control in the expanding sphere of cultural production and consumption by ' "capitalists" or "bureaucrats" ' (1988a: 224). Second, the term is employed to describe a world-view marked by pluralism, 'the futility of modern dreams of universalism', and a relativism of knowledge or dissipation of objectivity (1988a: 225–6; 1988b: 799). Finally, the concept of postmodernity is used to identify a 'fully fledged, comprehensive and viable type of social system', one which has replaced 'the classical modern, capitalist society and thus needs to be theorised according to its own logic' (1988b: 807, 811).

The advent of postmodernity as a 'world-view' is closely associated with transformations identified above as manifestations of an emerging sociological crisis. The dispersion of the 'orthodox consensus' which had continued to affirm the possibility of achieving a 'rational organisation of the human condition' (Bauman 1990a: 422) through the deployment of legislative forms of reason coincided with the emergence of a 'postmodern' sociology. However, if a combination of Garfinkel's ethnomethodology, phenomenological analyses derived from the work of Schutz, Wittgenstein's linguistic analyses, and Gadamer's hermeneutics constitutes a postmodern sociology it is one bereft of a concept of postmodernity. Because postmodern sociology is unable to generate a concept of postmodernity from within its own idiosyncratic terms of reference it is considered to be ill equipped to investigate postmodernity as a 'type of social reality with a place in history and social space' (Bauman 1988b: 805; 1989: 38). At best what postmodern sociology provides is an understanding of the tenuous, negotiated, constantly constituted character of social realities. It draws attention to the interminable labour of interpretation that is not only inescapable in social life, but is also constitutive of it.

In contrast to an 'interpreting' postmodern sociology Bauman proposes a sociology of postmodernity which would take seriously the possibility that a new 'fully-fledged comprehensive and viable type of social system' (Bauman 1989: 45–6) has emerged and simultaneously would seek to preserve the twin ambitions

of modernity (namely, increasing the volume of human autonomy
and the intensity of human solidarity) by recalling and reconstituting the 'emancipatory' objectives of sociological inquiry. A
number of significant transformations are implied in the idea
of postmodernity as a new type of social system, notably the
development of a 'post-full-employment' consumer society; the
increasing emancipation of capital from labour; important differences between the 'new' and the 'old' poor; and the inappropri-
ateness of recycled 1930s social analysis and political strategy
in contemporary conditions (Bauman 1988a, 1988b, 1989). The
argument is that consumer conduct, consumption, rather than
work or productive activity has become 'the cognitive and moral
focus of life, integrative bond of the society, and the focus of
systemic management' (Bauman 1989: 46). In such circumstances
it is the pursuit of pleasure through the consumption of commodities and services that has become a necessity, rather than self-
denial or the deferring of gratification. A corollary of which is
that complex and subtle forms of seduction have assumed increasing significance in processes of systemic reproduction and social
integration. The identification of transformations of this order
lend weight to the view that a redirection or refocusing of sociological analysis is now necessary. However, there are a number
of other related matters which still require clarification. In particular, does the proposal that it is necessary to move beyond a
'postmodern sociology' to a 'sociology of postmodernity'
(Bauman 1988a: 235; 1988b: 805; Featherstone 1988: 205) imply
a return to 'business as usual'? Sociology has been closely articulated with the 'practices and ambitions' of modernity and in so far
as the latter is 'undergoing profound change' Bauman suggests it
is unlikely that 'the business of sociology can go on "as usual".
There seems to be little in the orthodox lore of sociology which
can a priori claim exemption from re-thinking' (1989: 50). This
leads to a process of re-thinking directed towards possible new
'postmodern' objects of investigation, for example social processes and social movements; 'the increasingly apparent plurality
and heterogeneity of the socio-cultural world' (1989: 53); and
'social spaces beyond the confines of the nation-state' (1989: 56).
But it leaves the question of the adequacy of the procedures and
purposes of contemporary sociological inquiry in abeyance.

Bauman's remarks on the methodological and epistemological consequences of the dissolution of the orthodox consensus
and development of a postmodern sociology limited to the media-

ting activities of interpretation and translation between language games and forms of life, do tentatively suggest another possible option or strategy, namely for a sociology which continues to address 'modern concerns under postmodern conditions' (Bauman 1988a: 234–5). A sociology which continues to try to promote forms of autonomy and solidarity through a postmodern strategy that 'refers to values rather than laws; to assumptions instead of foundations; to purposes and not to "groundings" ' (1988a: 232). However, the implications for the practice of sociology of a postmodern shift from an 'onto-epistemological' tradition to a 'value-theoretical' tradition (Fekete 1988) have as yet to be fully explored.

The idea of the 'postmodern' is by no means new to sociological discourse. As I have already indicated, in the 1950s Wright Mills made the observation that the modern age is 'being succeeded by a post-modern period'.[9] Subsequently Berger *et al.* (1973) employ the term in connection with the idea of modernity having 'run its course' and Bell (1976) makes several critical references to the development in the 1960s of a postmodern temper or mood 'which carried the logic of modernism to its farthest reaches' (Smart 1990). The analyses I have discussed above are each concerned with related aspects of the transformation of modernity and their effects upon sociology. The modern epistemological configuration within which the human sciences emerged effectively determined that pluralism would be a constitutive feature of theory and method in sociology, and in the wake of the 'posthumanist' disarticulation of that configuration the diversity of standpoints has if anything increased. In addition there has been increasing reference to the need to reconsider, in the light of evidence on the impact of a range of socioeconomic, cultural and political changes on the organisation and experience of social life, whether society still constitutes the most appropriate focus or object of sociological inquiry. Whether these manifestations point to the existence of a 'postmodern condition' or to a 'new social and economic moment' (Lyotard 1986) remains an open matter. Certainly the debate over the transformation of modernity has crystallised a number of fundamental problems for sociological analysis. But whether 'postmodernity' is the most appropriate term to capture and explain the various changes identified continues to be a source of controversy.

NOTES

[1] Foucault comments that:

> The only thing we know at the moment, in all certainty, is that in Western culture the being of man and the being of language have never, at any time, been able to co-exist and to articulate themselves one upon the other. Their incompatibility has been one of the fundamental features of our thought.
>
> (1973: 339)

See also Hacking's (1988) discussion of the place of language in *The Order of Things*.

[2] Baudrillard makes several references to the influence of McLuhan's work (e.g. 1983b: 35, 100–103). See my discussion in *Modern Conditions, Postmodern Controversies* (Smart 1992).

[3] An example of such a conception of the social is provided by the work of Donzelot (e.g. 1979; 1988).

[4] For a discussion of the 'end of history' see Baudrillard (1987: 67–70; 1988b: 35–44).

[5] The parameters identified by Giddens are as follows:

(i) sociology is not simply an 'interpretative' endeavour, it produces 'accounts of social life which differ from those offered by social agents';

(ii) sociological generalisations to be validated by detailed empirical observation, however the former are in turn subject to modification through incorporation in social life;

(iii) while institutional constraints form and condition human conduct and associated outcomes, human behaviour is not to be explained simply in terms of the direct effect of 'social causes'; and

(iv) sociological concepts, theories and findings 'spiral in and out' of social life; they do not form an increasing corpus of knowledge (1987: 31–2).

[6] See Toynbee's earlier observations on the problematic status of the intellectual division of labour between sociology and anthropology (1954b: 188–9).

[7] For an address of the question of the articulation of state

and society see Donzelot (1988). See also the discussion of the state in Giddens (1985).

[8] See Giddens's discussion of the notions of 'society' and 'social system' (1984: xxvi–vii, 163–8).

[9] Wright Mills argues that the assumption derived from the Enlightenment of an 'inherent relation of reason and freedom' has become highly problematic and that our understandings of 'society and of self are being overtaken by new realities' (1970: 184).

3

Sociology, ethics and the present

What is it about present circumstances that has precipitated yet another series of re-appraisals of the practice of sociology? Is it 'that for the first time in history there exists the possibility, if not probability, of the *man-made* end of all human beings, of all life, of the planet itself'? (Wolff 1989: 321). The spectre of thermo-nuclear destruction and ecological devastation certainly continues to threaten the survival of humanity as a whole. But there are other aspects or elements of the present situation, other pressing problems and predicaments whose effects are more 'regional'. Specifically, I have in mind the dire problems of mass starvation and malnutrition, poverty and homelessness, and disease and ill health affecting substantial numbers, if not the majority, of people in the southern hemisphere, populations which have been relatively marginal within European and North American sociology. Other important features of the present, relatively neglected by modern forms of sociology preoccupied with contributing to the constitution of 'society', include the presence of armed struggles and military conflicts in formerly colonised territories, conflicts which in many instances follow directly from the installation of inappropriately constituted 'modern' nation-states, geopolitical unities which are at odds with longer-standing traditional, cultural, and/or tribal unities which have not only survived attempted processes of dissolution but now appear to be undergoing a regeneration. Signs of the reinvigoration of 'traditional' communities and 'local' identities are present on a global scale, across Europe and Asia, throughout the continent of Africa, in America, and in the region conventionally designated the Middle East. Here too there is very definitely a requirement to justify the practice of sociology. A need to recall the specific historical, cultural and geopolitical conditions of its emergence and development, that is post-Enlightenment in Western Europe, and to contemplate its deconstruction and reconstitution.

What appears to have led to the question of justification being raised in relation to sociology in present circumstances is that both its specific promise, and the more general promise of the Western 'project of modernity' of which it constitutes a part, namely a realisation of the 'values of personal autonomy and societal rationality' (Bauman 1987: 192) have yet to be fulfilled. But it is not simply a question of the project of modernity being incomplete, awaiting a future consummation. As I have indicated both the prospect and the desirability of its completion are in question. It is no longer possible to assume that a 'good' government and 'beneficial' transformation of reality will ultimately emerge from the rationalisation project of modernity. On the contrary, as Wright Mills cautions, '[r]ationally organised social arrangements are not necessarily a means of increased freedom – for the individual or for the society' (1970: 187). And given that the emergence and development of sociology as a distinctive form of inquiry is associated with the advent of Western modernity it follows that doubts about the latter needs must have implications for the sociological project.

JUSTIFICATIONS FOR SOCIOLOGY

From its inception sociology has been moved continually to justify its existence in various ways. The principal theme of legitimatory narratives has been of sociology developing, or advancing towards a more secure, certain, and orderly condition, in which theoretical, conceptual, and methodological variations are reduced in both scale and scope as 'a measure of scientific maturity' (Bottomore and Nisbet 1979: xv) is attained. This fiction has become increasingly difficult to sustain as the theoretical and methodological terrain of sociology has fragmented into a plurality of, in many cases incommensurable, approaches and positions. Following the collapse of the 'orthodox consensus' and the proliferation of incommensurable forms of theory and methodology the prospect of 'achieving a unified theoretical language for sociology' (Giddens 1987: 29) has receded. Rather than a sharpening of focus on an agreed and limited set of problems, the development of an accumulating body of knowledge, a reduction in the range of approaches employed within the field, and the achievement of an increasing degree of coherence, contemporary sociology presents us with dispersion, fragmentation, difference and disagreement. However, it is important not to exaggerate the extent of the change, important to avoid over-stating the reach and significance of the orthodox consensus. For diversity, to a degree, has been a feature of the undulating and variegated field of sociology from the beginning. The difference now is that sociology is addressing a wider 'assortment of ever-changing issues in a dazzling diversity of languages . . . [which] imply divergent if not incommensurable philosophical, moral and ideological standpoints' (Seidman 1990: 2). There have been a number of different views expressed on the current condition of sociology. I will briefly refer to two broad categories of response relevant to the matters under consideration here.

The first response has been to re-assert the necessity and to re-affirm the possibility of a foundationalist, naturalistically inclined, universalising modern sociology. We are advised that a standardisation of sociological concepts is long overdue and that a scientific 'discipline must adhere to some shared set of basic concepts referring uniquely and reliably to its domain of study' (Wallace 1991: 1). The promised benefits of standardisation are said to include a cumulative ordering of knowledge and the achievement of a sense of solidarity among sociologists. The objective is to transform sociology from a 'rabble of minitraditions sharing no identifiable common themes' to a 'discipline adhering to a single metatradition' (Wallace 1991: 1). Comparable sentiments concerning the virtues of universal epistemic rationales, general concepts and principles, and the possibility of 'constructing a comprehensive theory of social behaviour that is applicable to all times and places' (Haynor 1990) have been expressed recently in debates within the Theory Section of the American Sociological Association.

In contrast the second category of response takes issue with the standardising 'legislative' approach implied above and argues that sociology is a pluralistic, multi-level, reflexive discourse about social life articulated in terms of a number of different and, in important respects, discrete traditions (Alexander 1991). Given the characteristic features of sociological work – the reflexivity and circularity of social knowledge; the possibilities of exchange between lay and sociological concepts and understandings; and the problems of replication and control of variables – Giddens remarks that we 'must be sceptical of the ambition to achieve a professionally agreed-upon schema of theories and concepts in sociology' (1987: 31). However, scepticism here about the possibility of 'theoretical consensus' does not mean that anything goes, rather it represents a necessary coming to terms with the realities of social inquiry and the inescapable articulation of social knowledge with social life.

When Gouldner (1971) warned of an approaching crisis of Western sociology, a crisis exemplified by the 'entropy of functionalism', emergence of new forms of social theory, and increasing pressure to assist in 'practical problem-solving', he identified the 'beginning of a new period', the development of a new structure of sentiments, or new cultural mood. The analysis presented resembles an earlier diagnosis of the condition of the discipline advanced by Wright Mills (1970). Both exhort the social analyst to concentrate on the epoch in which they are living, their present, the salient characteristics of their own particular time, and they each imply that in so far as we are living in a time of transition the analytic task is made much more difficult. Our existing conceptions, understandings, and assumptions, derived from an earlier historical transition, are held to be unable to cope with the changing order of things. In brief, 'when they are generalised for use today, they become unwieldy, irrelevant, not convincing' (Wright Mills 1970: 184). Both Wright Mills and Gouldner identify the beginning of a new period and call for a reconstitution of sociology, a regeneration of the sociological imagination and a restoration of its promise, and the cultivation of a 'radical or neo-sociology' respectively. In each case a number of problems are addressed which anticipate the current concern articulated within sociology over the question of the possible emergence of a postmodern condition of knowledge, and/or spatio-temporal condition of postmodernity.

The justification to which modern sociology has conventionally aspired has been the amelioration or resolution of social problems, the provision of knowledge and technologies through which social forms and practices might be redesigned and reordered. Under conditions provisionally and somewhat ambiguously designated as postmodern this aspiration has continued to grow as further emphasis has been placed on the legitimation of research through performativity. What are the prospects for modern sociology justifying itself in a postmodern context? The non-economic problems identified by Gouldner as the focus of concern for modern sociology remain, but the social, cultural, economic, and political context in which sociology now finds itself is rather different. The current predicament is not that modern sociology is compromised by its 'role as market researcher for the Welfare State' (Gouldner 1971: 439), but rather that significant reductions in the scope and scale of the latter have diminished both the demand and the resources available for such forms of sociological research. The relative shift of responsibility for social integration from the state to the market, from repression to seduction, has undoubtedly made problems for modern sociology in so far as it has simultaneously reduced the scope for justification, limited the opportunities for sociology to demonstrate its value. However, if the troubles of modern sociology have increased with the development of 'postmodern conditions', so under duress has the commitment to the performativity principle. Contributing to the enhanced performativity of the social system remains a prominent form of justification for the practice of sociology, but it does not exhaust the possibilities. There are other sociologies and other possible justifications. Forms of sociology which are not directly implicated in the administrative extraction of knowledge and constitution of social technologies. Sociologies which cast doubt on both the feasibility and the desirability of the modern sociological project. Justifications which challenge the confinement of sociology to the technocratic task of optimising the performance of the social system.

SOCIOLOGY, INTERPRETATION AND CRITIQUE

Alternative forms of sociology and associated justifications have a long history within the discipline. Obvious examples would be forms of 'critical' sociological theorising which have been derived from Marxism and hermeneutic, or 'reflexive', styles of sociological analysis, their respective justifications being 'emancipation' and 'understanding'. Notwithstanding the possible existence of postmodern conditions these alternative forms continue to be invoked; they are still in play. Indeed it might be argued that under postmodern conditions these alternative forms have not come to an end, but rather have been reconstituted and developed, in order to address more adequately the changed circumstances and concerns of the time.

The condition of 'uneasiness and indifference' identified by Wright Mills as 'the signal feature of our period' (1970: 19) lies at the very centre of Kurt Wolff's discussion of the forms of sociology that might be considered justifiable in present circumstances. It is an uneasiness occasioned by the unprecedented gravity of the problems currently confronting humanity. An uneasiness about the justifiability, in present circumstances, of the 'dominant view of sociology' which is relatively indifferent to questions of existential meaning. The unprecedented character of the crisis of humanity necessitates in Wolff's view a different sociological response – one which involves a questioning of prevailing self-understandings of sociology, and a suspension of existing concepts and theories. The implication is that modern sociology shares some of the responsibility for the dilemmas we now confront. As Wolff comments, 'treating people as puppets, sociology repeats the treatment which many people more often than not experience and practise in our everyday world; sociology thus connives in a prevalent value judgement and in a by no means morally neutral activity' (1989: 337). In contrast there is said to be justification for two alternative kinds of sociology, a 'world-opening' or interpreting sociology and a 'critical' sociology, which place emphasis on the human subject and display a 'commitment to a good society'. Two possibilities come to mind here. One returns us to the conventional terrain and founding assumptions of the social sciences, namely that armed with knowledge about the social world, and a conception of a 'good society', we will be in a position to transform the world according to our design(s). Such a view cannot be sustained and is, in any event, at odds with the tenor and spirit of Wolff's analysis. The second, more appropriate and sustainable possibility is that since the practices of the social sciences necessarily depend upon or involve a double hermeneutic, then, as Giddens suggests, social scientists need to 'be alert to the transformative effects that their concepts and theories might have upon what it is they set out to analyse. Critical theory is not an option for social science . . . it is inherent in its nature' (1987: 71). Hence the need for a 'commitment to a good society'.

However, this does not settle matters. The debate over present conditions suggests that more is at stake, namely, as I have indicated earlier, the continuing relevance of 'society' as the object of sociological inquiry and reflection, and a related question, noted above, of the kinds of sociology, and the types of justification, which are possible under postmodern conditions.[1]

SOCIOLOGY UNDER POSTMODERN CONDITIONS

The history of sociology illustrates Touraine's observation that analyses of social life are 'transformed together with the realities which they try to grasp' (1989: 5). So, what types of sociology are possible under conditions of postmodernity? What kinds of justification are accessible to sociology under postmodern conditions? An acceleration of economic and technological change; associated transformations in the experience of space and time; a shift from production to consumption as the fulcrum of individual and social existence; the increasingly global scale of economic and cultural forms of life; and the (re)emergence of 'regional', 'ethnic' and traditional social divisions have rendered the idea of 'society' as a unity, equivalent to the geopolitical order of the modern nation-state, problematic as the focus for contemporary sociology. As Touraine comments, 'when people lived within a national . . . space, the nation was synonymous with society, but the obvious dissociation of these two realities in our era of economic and cultural internationalisation (accompanied by a reactive search for more immediate identities and communities) undermines the received image of society' (1989: 8). Whether the processes of economic and cultural globalisation and their diverse, complex corollaries constitute symptoms of the emergence of a 'radical' or 'high' modernity following 'the ever-more complete disintegration of the traditional world' (Giddens 1987: 29), or the development of a condition of 'postmodernity' – 'an aspect of a fully-fledged, viable social system' (Bauman 1989: 49), is for us to explore and debate.

The range of changes identified as symptoms of the development of postmodern conditions is not confined to the processes outlined above; a further significant factor is the difficulty, in the absence of 'the certitude of yesteryear', of providing an authoritative justification for intellectual activity, a difficulty which manifests itself in both a felt sense of anxiety and uneasiness, and a loss of status and resources. Whether the delegitimation of the grand narratives of knowledge ('the life of the spirit and/or the emancipation of humanity') and the predominance of the performativity criterion in knowledge production are 'sounding the knell of the age of the Professor' (Lyotard 1986: 53) is a moot point. Not so the loss of social status and material resources, or the related difficulty of justification. Indeed, the increasing difficulty of providing authoritative justification(s) for mainstream, 'orthodox' sociological practices – 'grand theory' and 'abstracted empiricism' (Wright Mills) and 'systems theory' and 'functionalist' social research (Gouldner) – both contributes to, and is exacerbated by the development of 'postmodern' forms of sociology, forms of sociology which place emphasis upon the tenuous, negotiable, meaningful, interpretive, and sociolinguistically constituted character of social life, upon the fragile 'tacit understandings' which constitute the insecure foundation of social life.[2] Postmodern sociology undermines the 'legislative-engineering' aspirations of modern sociology and 'casts the sociologist, with no need of further argument, into the role of the interpreter, of the semiotic broker with a function to facilitate communication *between* communities and traditions' (Bauman 1989: 39). The implication of which is that the justification for such a sociology is the adequacy of its 'translation' service, the extent to which it succeeds in bringing 'alien' communities or traditions into 'communicative contact', or is 'world-opening'.

But if 'postmodern' sociology begins with Garfinkel's ethnomethodology and Schutz's phenomenological sociology, and develops by way of Wittgenstein's idea of 'language games' and Gadamer's notion of the 'life world' as a 'communally produced and traditionally validated assembly of meanings' (Bauman 1989: 37), need it end there? Is there any scope for a 'postmodern' sociology which extends beyond the tasks of translation and mediation, a postmodern sociology which is more than ethnomethodologically indifferent? Is there scope for a postmodern sociology interested in determining 'why one definition of social reality becomes prevalent in one time, or place, or group, and another elsewhere' (Gouldner 1971: 391)? A postmodern sociology which is concerned with the processes of struggle through which social realities are defined, a 'regime of truth' or order of 'representations' established. Such a possibility is implied in the notion that postmodern sociology may give voice to cultures and communities which would otherwise 'remain numb or stay inaudible' (Bauman 1989: 39). This suggests a form of analysis which has as its central task the reactivation of disqualified, local, popular and illegitimate forms of knowledge, 'against the claims of a unitary body of theory which would filter, hierarchise and order them in the name of some true knowledge and some arbitrary idea of what constitutes a science and its objects' (Foucault 1980: 83). In brief a form of analysis that lays no claim to totality or universality. But to achieve this objective something more is required than a repetition of Garfinkel's disturbing demonstrations, the aim of which is to disrupt or breach the self-evidence on which our knowledges and practices are predicated. The requirement is for critical analyses of prevailing 'regimes of truth', analyses which explore 'the connections, encounters, supports, blockages, plays of forces, strategies and so on which at a given moment establish what subsequently counts as being self-evident, universal, and necessary' (Foucault 1981: 6). But, as I have already observed, if we take Foucault at his word we might question whether this type of analysis warrants the description 'postmodern'. In turn some analysts will undoubtedly question whether such an analysis constitutes sociology. The answer probably depends on the extent to which there is a willingness to consider changes within and between disciplines and to re-think the relationships between sociology and other cognate fields.[3]

One type of response to the several transformations referred to above has been to argue that they represent variations on a continuing theme, a manifestation of the recurring crisis of modern society. Changes are frequently conceptualised as merely symptoms of passing aberrations within a basically continuous modernity, rather than as traces of the emergence of a potentially new form of social life. The debate over the significance of contemporary social, cultural, economic, and political transformations extends from mainstream sociological inquiry through to the Marxist tradition, and in the case of the latter questions of justification have become especially acute because the analytic foundations and political strategies and objectives of Marxism are challenged by the idea of postmodern conditions. However, rather than regard the various signs of transformation simply as crisis inducing, disorganising disturbances or 'pathological aberrations' within modern society, we might treat them as manifestations of the development of new forms of social life, developments which may require a refocusing of sociological inquiry, but not necessarily a new justification. Consumption rather than production may have become the focus or centre of social existence, and seduction rather than repression may have become the predominant mechanism of system control and social integration, but the justification for doing sociology seems to continue to be 'a reason-led improvement of the human condition; an improvement measured in the last instance by the degree of human emancipation' (Bauman 1988a: 231). The question is, under present conditions, how can sociology contribute to a reason-led improvement of forms of human existence?

If contemporary sociology is to continue to contribute to an improvement of the human condition, then under changed conditions it may need to assume a different form. Appeal can no longer be made to 'guarantees' – to secure foundations, incontrovertible grounds, and law-like propositions – the conditions we encounter, conditions which may not be quite as novel as we are sometimes inclined to believe, require a different strategy for sociology, one involving what might be called an 'ethical turn', one which recognises 'the practical implications of the double hermeneutic' (Giddens 1987: 48). In short, there is a need for a sociology which recognises that knowledge of the social world 'alters its nature, spinning it off in novel directions' (Giddens 1990: 153), one which takes seriously the moral and political implications of its complex 'transformative consequences'.

AN ETHICAL (RE)TURN? Laurel

A number of factors are contributing to a redirection and/or reorientation of sociology. These include a broadening of the focus of inquiry from society and the nation-state to the social spaces within and beyond the forms of 'internal regionalisation' and 'modes of organisation that cross-cut national perimeters' (Giddens 1987: 34); to the increasing significance of 'social change and social movements' (Touraine 1989: 21); and to the impact of postmodern conditions upon a sociology which developed as 'a theory and a service discipline of modernity' (Bauman 1989: 51). However, the current reappraisal of sociology involves more than simply a change of focus or subject matter. It also contains a different conception and understanding of the relationship of sociology to the social world.

The social sciences in general have been unable to deliver on their promise to explain social phenomena in terms of law-like generalisations and, in consequence, to justify technicist claims to expertise in all things 'social'. But it might, in any event, be argued that this promise was, from the very beginning, misconceived or ill founded. In brief, that the modern sociological project derived from the Enlightenment, namely to explain social phenomena through law-like generalisations, and thereby to provide governmental and managerial social technologies, has not so much failed as, from the outset, been mistaken and thereby difficult, if not impossible, to justify. As Macintyre (1982) observes, the idea that the social sciences have failed in their task derives from a misunderstanding of their scope and potential, and in particular from a lack of appreciation of the systematic unpredictability of human affairs. A lack of predictability which derives, amongst other things, from the potential volatility and reality-generating capacity of (human) agency. From the fact that 'the unpredictability of certain of his (her) own future actions by each agent individually generates another element of unpredictability as such in the social world' (Macintyre 1982: 91).[4]

Ironically the uncertainty and unpredictability referred to is bound up with the very project which has sought to subject the social world to the order of a specific form of reason. The idea intrinsic to the project of modernity that knowledge of social life may facilitate prediction and control, that the optimum relationship between sociological knowledge and social life is one of instrumentality, is now difficult, if not impossible, to sustain. Recognition of the unavoidably reflexive relationship between the social sciences and the institutions, relations, and practices they analyse has problematised the modern assumption that the central objective of social knowledge is to generate technologies for ordering and controlling social life. As Giddens remarks 'the reflexivity of modern social life blocks off this possibility . . . The point is not that there is no stable social world to know, but that knowledge of that world contributes to its unstable or mutable character' (1990: 45). Contrary to Marx's thesis on Feuerbach it is not a question of interpreting the world *or* changing it, but rather of recognising that the forms of knowledge we produce, the interpretations we generate, necessarily contribute to the social world's transformation. And it is not simply the conditions in which we make our history that are not of our own choosing; the consequences of our collective conduct remain, for the most part, equally beyond our control, uncertain, at odds in many important respects with both our individual and our collective purposes. The conceptualisation of human agency as not only formed or located within social structures but in turn constitutive of them, together with the realisation that as sociologists draw upon lay concepts to generate analyses and understandings of social processes, so agents regularly appropriate sociological theories and concepts 'within their behaviour, thus potentially changing its character' (Giddens 1987: 30-1), returns questions concerning agency and subjectivity to the centre of sociological debate, and reminds us of the unavoidable implications of sociological work. The reconstitution of sociology is necessary to analyse the rapidly changing complexities of social life, and to understand the 'fluid, changeable social setting, kept in motion by the interaction of the plurality of autonomous and uncoordinated agents' (Bauman 1989: 51). But reconstitution is also necessary in so far as sociology is deeply implicated in its subject matter. Since the social sciences are unavoidably implicated in the constitution of the social world, the aim of a critical sociology necessarily becomes both to foster a 'developed conceptual awareness of the practical connotations of its own discourse' (Giddens 1984: 353), and open up new possibilities for thought and action. In circumstances where the 'ethically neutral institution' (Hennis 1988: 102) of the market is becoming increasingly significant to processes of societal integration and system control the longstanding objectives or aims of critical sociology, namely to problematise the self-evidence of prevailing forms of life and existing systems of thought, and to provide the 'kind of knowledge which may be used by human individuals in their efforts to enlarge the sphere of autonomy and solidarity' (Bauman 1988a: 233-4), remain crucial and need to be reinvigorated.

In a context where the process of modernisation seems to be precipitating an increasing separation of reason and morality, the social sciences in general, and sociology in particular, have a special responsibility. A responsibility to contribute to a restoration of the ethical basis of our relationship to ourselves and to others, and to counter the process of neutralisation to which the moral capacity of human agency has been subject in modern society, a process aggravated by both modern 'legislative' forms of sociology, which treat human agents simply as potential, if not actual objects of social technologies, that is as puppets or cultural dopes, and postmodern sociologies which display a disregard and indifference towards their moral subjects. The absence of the 'ethical . . . [as] the guiding value' (Rabinow 1986) has been identified as a consistent and problematic feature of modern society by a number of critics. Such a society provides 'a setting in which an orderly conduct of life is possible without recourse to the innate human capacity of moral regulation' (Bauman 1990b: 29), the corollary of which is the moral vulnerability of human beings to manipulation and to participation in forms of conduct, or practices, which are not subject to ethical considerations. Existing for the most part in the dense, impersonal, or faceless domain of 'the social', a virtual moral vacuum ordered through legal-rational mechanisms of government, human beings are constituted both as objects of forms of knowledge and subjects of associated therapeutic, managerial, and bureaucratic technologies which promise 'the manipulation of human beings into compliant patterns of behaviour' (Macintyre 1982: 71), but fortunately are unable to deliver.

It is no longer possible to attach any credence to the idea of secure epistemological foundations, or to the notion of political guarantees. Whether these and other related symptoms really warrant the description postmodern, or should instead be regarded as signs of the development of a 'radical' or 'high' form of modernity, is not decisive for my argument. My principal concern here is with the symptoms and their implications for the practice of sociology. In a context where the notions of reason, universality, and progress at the centre of the project of modernity are widely recognised to be attributes of a specific European cultural formation the idea of a progressive universal reason can no longer be sustained. And given the world is viewed as 'a plurality of heterogenous spaces and temporalities', and there is an associated 'acceptance of the plurality of cultures and discourses' (Heller and Feher 1988: 5) there is no scope for a redemptive politics. In such circumstances the objective of a critical-interpretive sociology becomes not the systematic accumulation of knowledge or the provision of social strategies, but the generation of a critique 'which does not attempt to fix the foundations for knowledge, to provide theory with a justification, or to defend reason, but to occasion new ways of thinking' (Rajchman 1985: 123). The aim of a critical-interpretive sociology is to challenge prevailing regimes of truth and associated relations of power, to contribute thereby to the processes through which 'things can be changed, fragile as they are, held together more by contingencies than by necessities, more by the arbitrary than by the obvious, more by complex but transitory historical contingency than by inevitable anthropological constraints' (Foucault 1982b: 35). In brief, to contribute to processes of change, not through the constitution of social technologies which might be employed to regulate or re-design social life, but by cultivating critical forms of sociological inquiry which recognise the implications of the unavoidably reflexive relationship between social analysis and social life. Implied in my argument is a sociological appropriation of Foucault's conception of critical inquiry, a conception which regards freedom as practical rather than ideal, and which emphasises the ethical import of knowledge, the contribution knowledge makes to processes of questioning, challenging, and transforming existing social institutions, social practices, and prevailing forms of identity.

Under present conditions the requirement is for critical forms of analysis which are alert to the open-ended and continually transformative capacity of modernity, analyses appreciative of the uncertainties, the risks and the dangers, associated with social and political transformations. In turn, what Giddens has justifiably described as a 'critical theory without guarantees' (1990: 155) needs to generate realistic conceptions of alternative preferable social futures, conceptions of good forms of social life that are 'limited neither to the sphere of the nation-state nor to only one of the institutional dimensions of modernity' (1990: 156). Finally it is necessary to balance or complement the emphasis generally placed upon 'emancipatory politics' within critical thought with a consideration of the increasing significance of 'life politics' grounded in an 'ethics of the personal' (Giddens 1990: 156–7), and exemplified by the growing importance of social movements preoccupied with aspects of individual self-actualisation. The latter signals a return to moral and existential concerns that have been marginalised, displaced or concealed not only by the core institutions of modernity (Giddens 1991) but also within 'much conventional socialist thought' (Therborn 1989).

The ethical turn, or return, to a 'value agenda' (Fekete 1988) derives its present impetus from a series of critical reflections upon modernity. Reflections which may be regarded as explicit contributions, or implicit responses, to the possible emergence of postmodern conditions. Whether we subscribe to the idea that our present is, in some sense, 'postmodern' is not of crucial significance. However, recognising the implications of the changes encompassed within the more sober formulations of the idea of the postmodern is vital, particularly for the practice of contemporary sociology. It is not simply a matter of us confronting 'new' conditions, although I would not wish to deny the existence and impact of qualitative changes arising from social, cultural, economic and political developments. But of at least equal significance is the growing sense that we have been both victims and perpetrators of deficient conceptions, if not damaging misconceptions of social conditions. To that extent problems have been, to a substantial degree, literally of our own making, our responsibility.

Critical analysis of 'the truth', of both our forms of thought and our 'selves', serves to alert us to the absence of epistemological and existential guarantees, and to detach 'the power of truth from the forms of hegemony, social, economic and cultural, within which it operates at the present time' (Foucault 1980: 133). It opens up the possibility, if not the necessity, of learning to live *without* inherited guarantees or securities, and *with* a 'pluralism of images and narratives of action, rationality and value'. Offers scope perhaps for contributing to the development of a 'livelier, more colourful, more alert, and one hopes, more tolerant culture' (Fekete, 1988: x–xi). In so far as it demonstrates the 'historicity of forms of experience' (Foucault 1986c: 334) and thought, and thereby allows us to recognise that there is scope for new forms of experience and new ways of thinking, that there are in short degrees of freedom, the study of sociology finds renewed justification.[5]

The circumstances and conditions we now encounter certainly appear more complex and challenging. We seem to live in between a state or condition of chaotic macro-interdependence and a plethora of seemingly inescapable 'particularities of places, characters, historical trajectories and fates' (Rabinow 1986: 258). We undoubtedly face a number of difficult problems, but we need to be careful not to overstate the gravity or uniqueness of our present circumstances. Anxieties about the future of the world and human existence are not peculiar to our present. Towards the end of the First Millennium Western culture was riven by fears and worries comparable to those current today, namely of the destruction of our habitat, the earth; the eruption of 'legions of the Devil' out of the East; and the prospect of epidemics which would wipe out the human race (Focillon 1970). The justification for sociology remains today, in part, as it always has been, namely offering a critical analysis of the conditions in which people find themselves in order that they may be better able to disengage from prevailing forms of experience and thereby constitute new forms of life. But if the justification for doing sociology remains, in one sense at least, the same, the (post)modern conditions under which it is practised are different. Increases in rationality are no longer considered to guarantee increases in freedom. There are no guarantees, certainties, or securities. The field of 'society' is in question as an appropriate, or valid, focus for sociological inquiry, particularly as we increasingly encounter a plurality of social spaces and subjects which do not 'refer to any ultimate unitarian basis' (Laclau and Mouffe 1985: 140). And given that the social is open, incomplete, and continually constituted through diverse articulatory practices, what may be difficult to justify is the distinctiveness, or specificity, of sociology as a practice, as a form of analysis, from say, philosophy, anthropology, history, and political economy. But, once again, that is not entirely a new problem.

NOTES

[1] Whether present conditions are in a definitive sense *post*modern is open to debate. I fully recognise the controversial and ambiguous status of the term (Smart 1990). As used here the term serves to capture provisionally the pervasive sense of the present as indeterminate and to draw attention to the potentially defective character of some of our analytic assumptions.

[2] The new forms of sociology which are considered to be synonymous with the collapse of the 'orthodox consensus' represent all social practices and processes, including science, as dependent upon tacit rules, taken-for-granted conventions, and arbitrary procedures (Gouldner 1971: 378–95).

[3] See for example Giddens's (1987) comments on the shifts in disciplinary boundaries affecting the social sciences in general and the relationship between sociology and anthropology in particular. A view endorsed by both Wolff (1989) and Bauman (1990a) in relation to sociology and philosophy.

[4] Macintyre identifies three other categories of systematic unpredictability affecting human affairs, namely:

→   (i) radical conceptual innovation;

→ (ii) the game-theoretic character of social life which involves the following: (a) the 'indefinite reflexivity' of game-theoretic situations; (b) the existence in social situations of 'imperfect knowledge'; and (c) the simultaneous presence of many different games and transactions; and

↪ (iii) the joker in the pack – pure contingency (Macintyre 1982: 89–95).

[5] As Raichman suggests,

> We are . . . 'really' free because we can identify and change those procedures or forms through which our stories become true, because we can question and modify those systems which make (only) particular kinds of action possible, and because there is no 'authentic' self-relation we must conform to.

>   (1985: 122)

4

Modern reason, postmodern imagination

Writing at the beginning of the century Weber characterised the 'fate of our times . . . by rationalisation and intellectualisation and, above all, by the "disenchantment of the world" ' (1970: 155). Although times have changed, few would disagree that the global diffusion of modern Western forms of reason has effected a disenchantment of the world. What that might involve, how the process of disenchantment described by Weber might now be interpreted, and what its consequences have been, has become a matter of re-appraisal (Whimster and Lash 1987).[1] In any event the globalisation of modernity, the global diffusion of Western rationality and the institutional forms associated with modern life, for example capitalism; industrialism; administrative coordination and surveillance associated with the nation-state; and control of the means of violence (Giddens 1990), constitutes merely one narrative, albeit a powerful one. Traditional communities and forms of life have indeed been dislocated, disturbed and disorganised by the corrosive consequences of modern rationalities, by the impact of the institutions of modernity upon traditional customs, practices, and beliefs. But there is another narrative present in a vestigial form in Weber's work which has recently received a much more explicit articulation, namely a disenchantment *with* modernity, articulated in one form in a 'post-modern' re-enchantment of the world.

Modernity has increasingly become subject to its own 'heretical imperative' (Berger 1980), vulnerable to the recognition of 'inconvenient' facts, the identification of unfulfilled promises, and the continuing existence of problems and dangers, if not exacerbated risks and threats. To what extent this critical condition constitutes a consequence of the development of modernity alone, represents an effect of the resistance, regeneration or reconstitution of traditional forms of life, and/or signifies an articulation of traditional and modern forms in various complex and unanticipated ways, is an issue currently exercising what I will describe as the 'postmodern' imagination.

REASONS TO BE CAUTIOUS: WEBER AND MODERNITY

The question of the fate of humanity under conditions of modernity is at the centre of Weber's work. For Weber the 'problematic of the modern mode of life – disenchanted, rationalised, disciplined' (Hennis 1988: 92) introduces a process of depersonalisation which increasingly affects all aspects of human life, undercutting in particular the possibility of an ethical conduct of life. The more the modern world is 'rationalised' the less the likelihood of living life in an ethically interpretable manner. The 'opacity of the world in which we are "placed" to ethical interpretation is the "fate" with which Weber's work struggles' (Hennis 1988: 102). It is the consequences or costs of the dissolution of personal and ethical relations synonymous with traditional forms of life that constitutes the central theme of Weber's exploration of the impact of modern reason on social conditions and human experiences.

The given, unconscious, and thus unquestioned 'unity' of the pre-modern world has been sundered by the dividing practices of modern reason. The development of modern purposively rational conceptions of the world has led to the relegation of religion and belief to the realm of the irrational. Weber comments that this has become 'more the case the further the purposive type of rationalisation has progressed' (1970: 281). The consequences of modern reason have subsequently become even more pronounced, the costs and the benefits a matter of continuing debate, and the misgivings tentatively articulated by Weber have been amplified and elaborated. Precisely when this 'modern age' commenced remains a matter of contention, with bids ranging from the fourth century and Augustine's reconstitution of a philosophy of progress (Kroker and Cook 1988) to the eighteenth-century Enlightenment and the advent of a 'tradition of reason', a tradition which Weber implies over-stated the scope and potential of reason, which promised more than could conceivably be delivered, and which ultimately contributed to the development of a 'charisma of reason' (Whimster and Lash 1987: 10). A charisma which has for some time now been on the wane. It is in Weber's fragmented sociological reflections on modern reason and its consequences that embryonic traces of the doubts and questions which have been developed in deliberations over the existence of a postmodern condition first receive sociological expression (Roth 1987). From the outset Weber is cautious about Western rationality, concerned to draw attention to its limits and limitations, and 'to show the tensions that existed in the relations between the processes of rationalisation as they existed, and still continue to do so' (Weiss 1987: 156). Specifically we might note the recurring difficulty which rational and methodical forms of life have had in satisfactorily answering questions about 'ultimate presuppositions', foundations, or grounds; the continuing problem of meaning in a 'disenchanted' modern world; and the accumulation of signs that the modern pursuit of mastery over all things through the continual refinement of calculating and purposive forms of rationality seems destined to remain unfinished, incomplete, and frustrated. Increasing rationalisation has not led to an increased general awareness of the conditions under which we live our lives, or to an enhancement of personal autonomy. On the contrary, increasing differentiation of fields of knowledge and an associated growth of specialists and professionals have precipitated an increase in forms of dependence (Illich 1978; Foucault 1981). Moreover, if the aim has been to submit all forms of life to calculation and control it is now clear that significant features of the social conditions we encounter remain incalculable and beyond external control. To that extent the modern world is less than completely disenchanted and, fortunately, modern subjects have yet to be reduced to the status of 'rational' objects.

For Weber it is clearly a moot point whether the process of rationalisation which has been a feature of Occidental culture and 'this "progress" to which science belongs as a link and motive force' have any meaning 'beyond the purely practical and technical' (1970: 139). The constant revolutionising and disturbance of all social relations, and the uncertainty and turmoil which constitute a necessary corollary of modernity represent, as we know from Marx and Engels (1968), the price to be paid for 'progress', the down-payment required to create the preconditions appropriate for a post-capitalist resolution of the 'social question' (Heller and Feher 1988). Weber, in contrast, considers the endless flux and turmoil associated with modernity, the constant transformation of culture, of ideas, forms of knowledge, prospects, possibilities, and problems, as the source of the meaninglessness which increasingly characterises modern existence. Modernity simultaneously creates the promise and the possibility, perhaps even a fleeting experience of satisfaction, but it is driven by an endless pursuit of innovation or change which creates restlessness, discontent, and dissatisfaction, and in consequence diminishes the experience and meaning of existence. As Weber remarks, 'the individual life of civilised man, placed into an infinite "progress" . . . placed in the midst of the continuous enrichment of culture by ideas, knowledge and problems . . . catches only the most minute part of what the life of the spirit brings forth ever anew, and . . . as such is meaningless' (1970: 139–40). Scientific rationality promised more, but it has simply offered 'artificial abstractions' which are unable to 'teach us anything about the *meaning* of the world' (1970: 142).

The context in which Weber was considering the consequences of modern conditions was one in which developing institutions and the routines of everyday life were challenging religion. At the risk of oversimplifying the contrast, the context in which I am attempting to explore the articulation of modern rationalities with what I am calling postmodern imaginations is one in which there is an increasing disenchantment with modernity, exemplified in particular by the challenge mounted by regenerated and reaffirmed religious systems of belief, and the apparently anomalous presence of postmodern conditions. Many old 'gods' have indeed ascended from their prematurely designated graves, but they are not all disenchanted, nor do they necessarily assume the form of impersonal forces as 'they strive to gain power over our lives and again . . . resume their eternal struggle with one another' (Weber 1970: 149). Refusing to accept the relativising consequences of modernity, the fundamentalist turn evident in each of the three monotheisms of Christianity,

Judaism, and Islam has promoted resistance to modern forms of life. Whether the religious movements which were thought to have been left behind by modernity have become the *avant-garde* of postmodernity is open to question (Sacks 1991). Less controversial is their contribution to the debate over the limits and limitations of modernity and the associated possible emergence of a mood or condition of postmodernity. The resurrection of the 'sacred' as a sphere of experience pertinent to modern forms of life, as a counter to the nihilism of the modern world and the 'vision of reason that brought this world into being', certainly constitutes a part of what has been described as the postmodern condition (Levin 1988).

The tension between religion and intellectual knowledge identified by Weber as a component of modernity persists, but the relation of forces has changed. Science continues to encounter claims that the social world is a meaningful and ethically orientated cosmos, but it is no longer so easy to consign intellectual approaches that pursue the meaning of occurrences or prioritise 'interpretive' over 'legislative' forms of reason, to the realm of the 'irrational'. That dividing practice is no longer sustainable. Weber clearly had a sense of the difficulties that were likely to arise:

> Science has created this cosmos of natural causality and has seemed unable to answer with certainty the question of its own ultimate presuppositions. Nevertheless science in the name of 'intellectual integrity', has come forward with the claim of representing the only possible form of a reasoned view of the world. The intellect, like all culture values, has created an aristocracy based on the possession of rational culture and independent of all personal ethical qualities of man . . . Worldly man has regarded this possession of culture as the highest good. In addition to the burden of ethical guilt, however, something has adhered to this cultural value which was bound to depreciate it with still greater finality, namely, senselessness – if this cultural value is to be judged in terms of its own standards.
>
> (Weber 1970: 355)

The idea that science represents the only reasoned view of the world is challenged by Weber. Rationalism means 'very different things' and the processes of rationalisation of conduct 'can assume unusually varied forms' (1970: 293). It is apparent that the rationalisation of world-views has developed in a number of different ways and has not led to a reduction of religious views of the world and a corresponding unproblematic 'increase in instrumentally rational forms of conduct graded by modern "value-free" science' (Mommsen 1987: 38). Religious world-views have not disappeared, on the contrary, as I have suggested above, they continue to exert a significant influence on the course of social development. A comparable conclusion is implicit in Gellner's work, in particular in observations on the limits of modern reason, notably that 'rationality dependent on the division of labour has transformed our world, but will never reach those all-embracing, inherently multi-strand choices between incommensurate alternatives' (1988: 210). In so far as this is the case the modern project is destined to remain perpetually unfinished, its realisation continually frustrated by 'residual' and 'irrational' forms that obstruct its quest for order (Bauman 1991a).

Rather than an inexorably ascendant or progressively rational social order, designed according to the cumulative wisdoms of modern Western civilisation, we inhabit a social world which has become increasingly disorientated and disturbed by the knowledge that it is 'committed to practising a rationality that is unfortunately crisscrossed by intrinsic dangers' (Foucault 1982a: 19). The effects of bewilderment and experiences of vertigo induced by the 'revolving door of rationality . . . its necessity . . . indispensability, and . . . intrinsic dangers' (Foucault 1982a: 19) may lead us to pursue more vigorously the receding promise of modernity. But it may also occasion a reconsideration of modern reason and inadvertently, or otherwise, provide scope for the cultivation of the 'postmodern' imagination.

IN THE SHADOW OF ENLIGHTENMENT

Concern about modernity and its consequences, inaugurated by Nietzsche and elaborated by Weber, has become increasingly prominent and is now pervasive. Nietzsche wondered where our modern world belonged, 'to exhaustion or ascent?' (1968: 48). The question continues to haunt us, albeit in a more aggravated context, one in which exhaustion, environmentally and experientially speaking, appears to have reached a more 'advanced' stage. Indeed, we seem to be increasingly confronted, if not overwhelmed by such questions. Where once we might have considered ourselves to be in possession of secure answers and solutions we now encounter doubts and questions. It is this process of questioning of modern resolutions that has been diagnosed as symptomatic of the existence of a 'post-modern' condition, the argument being ·that modernity only becomes 'visible . . . from the moment in which . . . the mechanism of modernity distances itself from us' (Vattimo 1988: 103). However, as my earlier comments indicate, the idea that a critical analytical purchase on modernity requires, or assumes, the existence of a condition of 'postmodernity' is open to dispute.

The question of modernity and its consequences is effectively a question of the post-Enlightenment development of Western civilisation and the rationalising project with which it has been articulated.[2] Since the eighteenth century there has been a prominent assumption that increasing rationality is conducive to the promotion of order and control, achievement of enhanced levels of social understanding, moral progress, justice, and human happiness. The pursuit of order, promotion of calculability, fabrication and celebration of the 'new', and faith in 'progress' have been identified as pivotal features of modernity. However, modernity, in turn, has become the focus of increasing critical reflection in the course of the twentieth century. The benefits and securities assumed to be a corollary of the development of modernity have become matters of doubt, the possibility of their realisation, if not their desirability, the subject of question and criticism as faith in the doctrine of progress has been dissipated.

What are we to make of these developments? As modernity has become subject to critical analysis, to its own heretical imperative, so in turn its sacred idols have been profaned, its 'prejudices and opinions . . . swept away' (Marx and Engels 1968: 83). We are no longer so easily deceived, or 'led astray', by the illusory logic of innovation, development, progress (Nietzsche 1968: 55). One response to which, exemplified in its strongest form by Habermas, has been to argue that we now encounter a strategic choice, either 'hold fast to the intentions of the Enlightenment . . . or . . . give up the project of modernity as lost' (1987: 326–7). Habermas is intent on defending the project of modernity from 'antimodern' and 'postmodern' criticisms, positions which are conceived to rob 'a modernity at variance with itself of its rational content and its perspective on the future'

(1987: 396). In particular Habermas seeks to preserve the primacy of modern reason by contributing to the development of an understanding of the world that may claim to have identified universal structures of human existence, universal norms for human action, and thereby, to have achieved universal validity (Dreyfus and Rabinow 1986).

Acknowledging the existence of a series of social, cultural, and political problems which have arisen with modernity McCarthy argues that there is a 'need to subject these phenomena to careful analysis if we wish to avoid a precipitate abandonment of the achievements of modernity. What is called for, it might be argued, is an enlightenment suspicion of enlightenment, a reasoned critique of Western rationalism' (1984: v–vi). To which there can be few, if any, major objections. The question is, however, whether an enlightenment suspicion of modern Western reason and its claims is to be found in Habermas's attempt to uphold and complete the project of modernity. Where enlightened suspicion and reasoned critique are present in Habermas's work they are directed almost entirely to the pathological consequences of 'capitalist modernisation'.

In contrast to the alternatives constituted by Habermas of either attempting to live up to the promise of the Enlightenment, or abandoning the project of modernity, a third possibility is evident, one embodied in a range of other analyses. In a series of diverse studies which explore the history of modern rationalities (Foucault), the politics of modern and postmodern conditions (Heller and Feher), the (post)modern experience, and problem, of living with contingency and ambivalence (Bauman), and the complex consequences of, and possible alternatives to modernity (Giddens), the question of Enlightenment and the project of modernity is approached, with varying degrees of explicitness, more openly, critically, and imaginatively than is possible within a project whose parameters are fixed from the outset by a felt need to defend and promote what appears to be constituted as a singular modern reason.

Above and beyond a number of significant differences in style, orientation, and focus, what each of the respective 'third category' of analyses to be considered here share is an evident willingness to address the possibility that the pursuit of order and control, promotion of calculability, affirmation of the 'new', preoccupation with 'progress' and other features intrinsic to modernity, are necessarily articulated with a simultaneously constituted range of additional experiences and conditions which are conceived negatively, as problems, namely the risk of chaos, the persistent presence of chance or threat of indeterminacy, and the increasing incidence of ephemerality and its *alter ego*, the seemingly inexorable growth of dissatisfaction (Heller and Feher 1988; Giddens 1990; Bauman 1991a). One implication of the above is that problems are not so much remedial 'abnormal' effects of a particular historical perversion of modernity, of its 'pathological' capitalist form, as consequences of the complex practices, institutional dimensions, and associated experiences inaugurated within Western Europe approximately two hundred years ago, and subsequently dispersed via a process of globalisation. In brief, they constitute consequences of modernity *per se*, that is of the only historically existing form known to us, 'modernity as a brand-new experiment . . . that is still in its period of trial and (grave) error' (Heller 1990b: 4). And increasingly in question.

Opening up the question of modernity and its consequences does not inexorably lead one to have to make a choice between an endorsement or a betrayal of the Enlightenment. We can refuse Habermas's gambit. As Foucault reminds us, it is not a matter of 'either accept the Enlightenment and remain within the tradition of its rationalism . . . or . . . criticise the Enlightenment and then try to escape from its principles of rationality' (1986a: 43). We can contribute to the making of our history, but we also know, after Marx, that we cannot do so under circumstances of our own choosing. Whether we are drawn to the light or hide ourselves in the shadows we remain, to a certain extent at least, both subjects of, and subject to the Enlightenment. One aspect of the question is then our connection to the Enlightenment, an aspect which I will pursue, albeit briefly, through Foucault's work.

In a sense the connection is already embodied in the very exercise on which I have embarked, namely a recognition of the possibility of an interrogation of the present. One way of understanding our continuing indebtedness to the Enlightenment is in terms of our perpetual, and necessary, return to the question of the present – 'what is my present? What is the meaning of the present? . . . Such is, it seems to me, the substance of this new interrogation on modernity' (Foucault 1986b: 90). But to say that our connection to the Enlightenment is embodied in the continuing presence, if not necessity, of a critical ontology of the present is to fast-forward to the conclusion. How does Foucault get there? Foucault argues that a number of paradoxes have led us back to the question of Enlightenment. Modern reason makes universal claims yet has developed in contingency, it constitutes a reason whose 'autonomy of structures carries with itself the history of dogmatisms and despotisms' (Foucault 1978: xii). The question of Enlightenment has returned for three key reasons, namely the increasing importance assumed by scientific and technical rationality in social, economic and political life and an associated concern about the uneven consequences which have followed; the growing realisation that a socioeconomic revolution cannot deliver on its promise to conclude the 'history of all hitherto existing society' (Marx and Engels 1968: 79); and finally, because post-colonial populations have begun to 'ask the West what rights its culture, its science, its social organisation and finally its rationality itself could have to laying claim to a universal validity' (Foucault 1978: xii). It is the articulation of questions such as these that has allowed analysts to speculate about the steady accretion of postmodern forms of life. But that is not Foucault's declared position, notwithstanding Hoy's (1988) powerful argument to the contrary.

Acknowledging that 'modernity as a question' has a history, Foucault comments that it is no longer necessary to pose it in terms of an 'axis with two poles, antiquity and modernity' (1986b: 90). Rather than conceive of modernity as an epoch 'preceded by a more or less naive or archaic premodernity and followed by an enigmatic and troubling "postmodernity" ' (1986a: 39), modernity may, more appropriately, be envisaged as an *attitude*, a way of relating to contemporary reality. This involves much more than an accommodation to the disruptions, discontinuities and forms of perpetual motion intrinsic to modern life. It is not 'simply a form of relationship to the present, it is also a mode of relationship that has to be established with oneself' (1986a: 41). For Foucault this represents a critical orientation to the present, a form of critical analysis derived from the work of Kant which reflects upon the limits within which our forms of knowledge, social practices, and modes of subjectivity are constituted, an analysis which transgressively asks, 'in what is given to us as universal, necessary, obligatory, what place is occupied by whatever is singular, contingent, and the product of arbitrary constraints?' (1986a: 45). It is precisely this characteristic of critical reflexivity that is identified by Giddens as symptomatic of the fact that we are living through a period of 'high' or 'radicalised modernity' (1990: 149, 163).

Whereas Foucault is unwilling to refer to modernity as an epoch, or era, suggesting instead that it is more appropriate to explore the various ways in which 'the attitude of modernity, ever since its formation, has found itself struggling with attitudes of "countermodernity" ' (1986a: 39), the other analyses to be considered here incorporate into their critical ontologies of the present a consideration of the structures and experiences associated with modern forms of life and, in turn, explore the doubts, uncertainties and problems which have been attributed to modernity and conceived to be symptomatic of the possible emergence of a condition of postmodernity.

MODERNITY AND ITS CONSEQUENCES

The consequences of modernity are manifold and far from exhausted, for modernity has by no means run its course. The consequences identified follow from the way in which modernity is conceptualised. For Foucault, as I have noted above, modernity is equated with an attitude, a way of relating to ourselves, others, and the conditions of existence we encounter, reproduce, and transform. The prevalence of a critically questioning, reflexive orientation, or modern attitude towards the present is evident in the identification of more and more areas of our existence as subject to 'the influence of history', an influence which 'introduces discontinuity into our very being' (Foucault 1977a: 153–4), makes it amenable to deconstruction and reconstitution and in consequence renders being or existence open to being different. Such an attitude does not imply, or guarantee, a progressive or positive outcome, a resolution of prevailing problems and difficulties, or the constitution of a 'higher' form of life; rather, it seems to represent for Foucault the way we are, the way in which we increasingly experience the complex processes that constitute and reconstitute our existence. Implicit in such a notion are the characteristics of ambivalence, contingency, and reflexivity integral to the other analyses of modernity and its consequences to be considered below.

If we take modernity to be a form of relationship to the present which was inaugurated with the Enlightenment then it may be argued that analytically it continues to represent a relative novelty, that it is 'still an abstraction in the early phase of the process of "concretisation" ' (Heller 1990b: 4). The interrogation of modernity, the recognition that yesterday's 'modern' resolutions are frequently the source of today's 'modern' problems, and the realisation that the passage of time and, what is often conceived to be its corollary, the quantitative accumulation of information and knowledge, are not able to render modern conditions more transparent because they simultaneously represent a form of 'interference' with the conditions themselves, have been identified as symptoms of a 'post-modern historical consciousness' (Heller 1990b: 6), 'the passage of modernity into its postmodern stage' (Bauman 1991a: 244), and, in contrast, of a 'radicalising of modernity' which indicates that 'we have entered a period of high modernity' (Giddens 1990: 52, 176).

It would be misleading to make too much, at this stage, of the contrasting terms employed to describe the continuing transformation of modernity, for there is a substantial degree of common ground between the respective positions identified. For example, modernity is regarded as a 'double-edged phenomenon' (Giddens 1990: 7), simultaneously a source of benefits and costs, satisfactions and dissatisfactions, securities and risks, opportunities and limitations. Modernity appears like a roller-coaster fuelled by perpetual oscillations between promised, and for some, some of the time, briefly realised moments, perhaps even 'significant niches of satisfaction' (Heller and Feher 1988: 11), amidst more sustained periods and experiences of discontent and dissatisfaction. Modernity presents itself as order, but its necessary corollary is disorder or chaos. In brief 'existence is modern in so far as it contains the *alternative* of order and chaos . . . [for] the negativity of chaos is a product of order's self-constitution: its side-effect' (Bauman 1991a: 6–7).

In pre-modern societies contingency is associated with the general condition of human existence – 'every person is thrown into a particular world by the accident of birth' (Heller and Feher 1988: 15) – and in consequence is experienced as fate. With modernity our relationship to our conditions of existence, our time and place, are transformed. An acceptance of fate is displaced by experience of the contingent character of the contexts in which we find ourselves:

It is not only being 'here' or 'there' that is conceived as contingent, so too is *the individual's relation* to a particular place and time as a mere 'context' . . . Put simply,

from a modern point of view, particular social arrangements and institutions can just as well exist as *not* exist.
The world into which people are born is no longer seen
as having been decreed by fate but as an agglomerate of
possibilities.

(Heller and Feher 1988: 17)

In a world which claims to be able to offer increasing scope for
choice, one potential choice, at least, has to be excluded, namely
the possibility of putting an end to the contingent character of
modern existence. Modernity appears to require us to live with
contingency, to cope with or to reconcile ourselves to conditions
which, whilst pretending to order, regulation, and necessity-by-
design have, in some far from final instance, to admit the persistent presence of contingency. Contingent existence is experienced
as 'existence devoid of certainty' (Bauman 1991a: 236). The
problem is how to respond to the presence and threat of uncertainty. In the absence of any predictable, safe, orderly havens
in which we can seek shelter from the turbulence and turmoil of
uncertainty, what are the options? Certainly not a reinvigorated
attempt to fulfil the modern project, which would surely deliver
more of the same. One alternative which has been proposed is
to try to 'eliminate contingency by transforming it into destiny'
(Heller and Feher 1988: 26). This seems to require us to regard
the actualisation of some of the diverse possibilities which have
constituted the various contexts in which we have lived and
reflected upon our existence as optimal outcomes, embodied in
and secured through our choices and actions. Such a strategy
may indeed relieve the anxiety which frequently accompanies an
awareness of the extent to which our existence has become subject to contingency. And it may allow us to feel that we have
made a mark, or left a trace on the world in which we live.
But any feelings of satisfaction within what remains, not only a
'dissatisfied society', but in many significant respects an unsatis-
factory one as well, ought perhaps to be tempered by the possibility that marks may be removed and traces erased.

If it is the pursuit of self-determination in cooperation with
others that 'best allows the transformation of our contingency
into destiny' (Heller and Feher 1988: 27), it is necessary to
recognise that such a strategy will not so much eliminate contingency as offer, at best, momentary relief from it, as self and
others act to shape their destiny and then reflect upon their

participation in the actualisation of one of the available possibilities open and known to them. The exercise of self-determination requires an awareness of the existence of options and possibilities, a sense of the relative openness in which conduct is both constituted and, in turn, constituting of other possibilities. In other words self-determination requires a degree of indeterminacy concerning present and future conduct. In short the absence of certainty constitutes the space in which self and others can make their marks, or leave their traces. The diverse contexts and fluctuating circumstances in which we find ourselves, and may attempt to (re)constitute ourselves as subjects, as selves able to recognise and take advantage of the potential for self-determination made possible by the absence of necessity, are themselves subject to contingency. It is the contingent character of aspects of the present in which we act that offers the possibility of self-determination. In so far as this is the case it is not the elimination of contingency that we should be seeking as much as the constitution of the conditions in which it becomes possible for people to exercise self-determination in the face of contingency. A task which begins with an acceptance of contingency as an intrinsic feature of both the modern self and modern society. Accepting 'that certainty is not to be' (Bauman 1991a: 244), that we live in and with contingency, does not represent a loss, for the promises of certainty were from the outset unrealisable. It is this question of how we cope with the consequences of living with contingency that has simultaneously troubled modern sensibilities and stimulated postmodern imaginations.

Modernity has a number of paradoxical features and consequences which now appear to permeate virtually all aspects of our existence. Reflecting on the difficulties of trying to cope with the 'juggernaut of modernity' Giddens cautions that

> so long as the institutions of modernity endure, we shall never be able to control completely either the path or the pace of the journey. In turn, we shall never be able to feel entirely secure, because the terrain across which it runs is fraught with risks of high consequence. Feelings of ontological security and existential anxiety will coexist in ambivalence.

(Giddens 1990: 139)

The resistance of things to our ordering practices and the associated experience of a lack of control as a problem contribute to the growing ambivalence identified as a corollary of modernity. Contingency, ambivalence, and a seemingly inexhaustible capacity to transform seductive prospects for satisfaction into frustrating experiences of dissatisfaction appear to be bound up with modernity, an intrinsic feature of modern existence. Difficulties of this order are taken to signify the need for further extensions or enhancements of modern practices, or, more ambitiously, a mission to retrieve the 'rational' promise of modernity from its historical perversion. In other words dissatisfaction, uncertainty, disorder and failure to achieve intended outcomes serve to promote more of the same, to revitalise the quest for satisfaction, control, order and the achievement of programmed goals. As Baudrillard acknowledges '[t]he problem has always been to create order out of supposed disorder, to produce and support movement, to sustain and produce meaning. This is what haunts us; it is our ideal' (1990: 147).

With the extension of the practice of reflexivity to modernity itself the assumption that problems and difficulties will be alleviated, if not resolved, through a continuing revision of the modern formula, has been challenged. But what does the process of interrogation to which modernity has become increasingly subject signify? Is 'the fading of self-deception a final fulfilment, emancipation, or the end of modernity?' (Bauman 1991a: 232). Does it represent a radicalisation of modernity, or is it more appropriate to consider it a symptom of a 'postmodern' turn? And if the latter, where might that turn be taking us?

MODERN CONDITIONS, POSTMODERN RESPONSES

If there are respects in which the positions briefly referred to above present a range of comparable observations on modernity and its consequences, there are simultaneously clear indications that substantial degrees of difference exist over the question of an appropriate conceptual designation for the social, cultural, and political conditions which now prevail, and to which our analyses needs must respond. For two of the positions, exemplified by Foucault and Giddens respectively, 'modernity' continues to be an appropriate designation for the present. But whereas Foucault's observation, that our analytic efforts should be directed towards trying to 'find out how the attitude of modernity, ever since its formation, has found itself struggling with attitudes of "countermodernity"' (1986a: 39), effectively consti-

tutes a dismissal of the notion of the 'postmodern', as of little
relevance for an understanding of contemporary conditions, Giddens, whilst arguing strongly that the conditions we encounter
represent the consequences of a process of 'radicalisation of
modernity', also entertains the idea of a possible future 'postmodern order' or system. As I have noted above, in this instance
postmodernity represents an imaginary social future, a project,
a model of a possible form of social life beyond modernity, one
created in 'the light of a framework of utopian realism' (Giddens
1990: 156, 163).

In contrast there are, as I have intimated, other analyses of
modernity and its consequences which suggest that it has become
necessary to generate and deploy a conception of postmodernity
in order to achieve an adequate understanding of contemporary
conditions. Accordingly we can find references being made to 'a
new outlook, a category which allows one to recognise the satu-
ration of a way of thinking and living, a category allowing the
recognition of a precarious moment situated between the end of
one world and the birth of the next . . . [T]he outlook of postmodern sociality' (Maffesoli 1990: 90–1); the appearance of
'unmistakeable trends of postmodern politics' (Heller and Feher
1988: 3); and new problems and possibilities, constraints, choices
and responsibilities illuminated by the 'postmodern' exposure of
modernity (Bauman 1991a). I will confine my comments here
to the postmodern responses to modern conditions and their
consequences outlined in the related works of Heller and Feher
on postmodern politics and Bauman on the task of coping with
the postmodern challenge.

In both cases postmodernity is presented as a way of relating
to modernity, literally a consequence of its consequences, a
response to the unfulfilled promises, thwarted hopes, and disturbing dilemmas that now have to be faced without the solace of
anticipated, if not guaranteed future resolutions. It is not that
nothing can be done, that present problems are conceived to be
necessarily impervious to future resolutions, but that problems
do not admit of quick technical fixes, and moreover that there
can be no final resolution to the dilemmas and difficulties
encountered in social life. Accordingly postmodernity is
described as 'not a new era' and as 'in every respect parasitic
on modernity; it lives and feeds on its achievements and on its
dilemmas' (Heller and Feher 1988: 10–11), and again as

no more (but no less either) than the modern mind taking a long, attentive and sober look at itself, at its condition and its past works, not fully liking what it sees and sensing the urge to change. Postmodernity is modernity coming of age . . . looking at itself at a distance rather than from inside, making a full inventory of its gains and losses . . . Postmodernity is modernity coming to terms with its own impossibility; a self-monitoring modernity, one that consciously discards what it was once unconsciously doing.

(Bauman 1991a: 272)

Sober and cautious claims which invite us to consider the prospect of a more modest modernity, not, I should emphasise, a new postmodern age.

The portrayal of postmodernity as a form of historical consciousness, a mentality, or attitude, leaves scope for consideration to be given to the question of the respects in which postmodern ways of relating to the world are formed and embodied in social life, and further may contribute to its restructuring. It has been suggested that the postmodern political condition is premised upon the demise of 'grand narratives' and an associated abandonment of redemptive forms of politics, a political and cultural campaign against ethnocentrism, and its corollary an 'acceptance of the plurality of cultures and discourses' (Heller and Feher 1988: 5). In respect of one prominent, increasingly challenged, yet not quite totally abandoned form of redemptive politics, namely socialism, it is hard to dispute that 'as a "new formation" transcending modernity [it] is a conceptual mythology' (Heller and Feher 1988: 117). Rather than constituting a new social and political space, socialism presents a rearrangement of the furniture of modernity as the solution to all social issues and problems. The complex histories of the societies of 'actually existing socialism' have taught us that the institutional changes which socialism might be able to deliver will not resolve all social issues, and this hard lesson has contributed to the erosion of socialism's 'grand narrative' status. The devaluation of socialism as the imaginary universal alternative progressive form of life to a problematic capitalist modernity and the related proliferation of postmodern social and political conditions, embodying pluralism and diversity, and manifest, for example, in relations of difference between cultures, authentic celebrations of otherness, and a denial of universals, make it necessary for us to consider how communities and peoples might be held together both 'locally', that is as relatively self-determining cultural and geopolitical 'unities', and 'globally', that is in relationships of difference articulated in complex solidary and flexible organisational forms.

A comparable form of response to the taxing challenges of living with contingency, with facing up to postmodern conditions, in cooperation with and in consideration of others, and in ways which might allow us to take advantage of the opportunities, as well as cope with the threats, risks, and dangers they simultaneously embody, informs Bauman's series of critical reflections on modernity and its consequences. Postmodern conditions are identified in a wide range of contexts and responses in contemporary social, cultural, political, and economic life. Intellectual disaffection with the modern goal of rationally engineering the good life; associated doubts about the feasibility, desirability, and relevance of global projects, particularly in a context where there are now recognised to be a plurality of cultures and discourses articulated with new, transient forms of local–global relations; evidence of a shift in relative significance or weight from repression to seduction in the reproduction of social life; and the experience of fragmentation and dislocation of both identity and community, following the acceleration of communications, over-production to excess of cultural products, information and meanings, and absence or discrediting of reliable reference points, secure standards, stable criteria, fixed forms, accepted authorities, guarantees, foundations and so on, may all be regarded as manifestations of a complex condition of postmodernity. The irretrievable loss of trust in the project of modernity and its ability to manage, enhance and ultimately to fulfil human potential, raises the prospect of more responsibility being restored to human agency. If we are to limit, or avoid, a paralysing nostalgia for the lost promise of modernity; if postmodern conditions are to be received and experienced as providing opportunities, in short turned to individual and collective advantage, then it is necessary to respond positively, with imagination, to the prospect of living *without* securities, guarantees and order, and *with* contingency and ambivalence.

POSTMODERN IMAGINATION

The prospect of living without certainty or necessity may cause us to respond with fear, anxiety, and insecurity, but equally it allows us to live with imagination and responsibility. Contrary to the responses of critics who have equated postmodernity with a reactionary or conservative form of politics (Habermas 1981; Callinicos 1989) there is no singular, predetermined or necessary postmodern political agenda. Irritatingly for those who require their targets to declare themselves either 'for' or 'against', it is increasingly evident that postmodernity presents 'a double face like Janus' (Heller and Feher 1988: 7), in effect that it constitutes a site, space, or clearing for political possibilities, rather than a distinctive political strategy.

It is sometimes suggested that the idea of postmodernity necessarily means 'anything goes'. But, *if* under conditions of postmodernity anything may go, it is not the case that any, or every thing does go, has to go, or has to be accepted. Living in a world of difference a measure of epistemological and ethical relativism appears to be inescapable, and at times this is equated with the idea of 'anything goes'. The fear of 'anything goes', of a chaos of (in)difference, arises in the context of an apparent loss of the prospect of order, certainty, and security. However, as I have already suggested, in practice little has been lost, for the promise of order, certainty, and security associated with the advent of modernity is necessarily articulated with the threat of chaos, indeterminacy, and risk. 'Anything goes' may also be taken to be a somewhat inflated invitation to contribute to the realisation of some possibilities rather than others, an indication that there is indeed a degree of scope for self-determination, that things can be changed. In short, an invitation to move beyond fate, or 'a feeling that things will take their own course anyway . . . [a feeling that] reappears at the core of a world which is supposedly taking rational control of its own affairs' (Giddens 1990: 133), to assume responsibility with others for the shaping of our destiny.

If the debate about postmodernity commences with a conception of the paradox intrinsic to modernity, it does not end there. Rather it extends to questions of 'new forms of subjectivity . . . [and] practices of the self in a postmodern world' (Levin 1988: 20), to alternative forms of postmodern politics, and the shape a future postmodern social order might assume. Whether it is

Foucault's notion of an 'aesthetics of existence' and the associated idea of politics as an ethics; Heller and Feher's contention
that we may be able to transform our lives from contingency into
destiny by satisfying the need for self-determination; Bauman's
caution concerning the need to nurture 'solidarity' to counter
the tendency 'for postmodern tolerance to degenerate into the
selfishness of the rich and powerful' (1991a: 257); or the somewhat different 'futuristic' conception of postmodernity outlined
by Giddens (1990), namely an institutionally complex post-scarcity, democratic and demilitarised social order which has achieved
a 'humanisation of technology', the forms of subjectivity and
community, and the social relations and practices that are
implied, remain indeterminate, and necessarily so.

What then of modernity? Can it endure? What are its
chances? Questions such as these are postmodern for they are
'posed to modernity from the point of view of post-modern
historical consciousness' (Heller 1990b: 6). They come not from
somewhere beyond modernity, from another time or place, but
from reflections on modernity. Reflections on a modernity alleg-
edly deprived, or better relieved, of its 'logic of development',
its twin unfounded assumptions of inexorable 'progress' and
'overcoming' (Vattimo 1988). It is in this sense that the idea of
postmodernity offers a 'chance of modernity' (Bauman 1991a:
257), a chance of a more modest modernity, an inherently reflexive modernity. A modernity which is acknowledged to face continually the necessity and difficulty of reconciling preservation or
defence of the central modern value of freedom with the forms
of difference and dissension that are increasingly recognised to
be inescapable and, in some cases at least, positive expressions
of it. Implied here is a sense that the survival of modernity
necessitates acceptance of 'the heterogeneity of dissensions' as
the only consensus likely to succeed and/or be sustainable
(Bauman 1991a: 251); accommodation to the transient and fluctuating character of communal forms of life experience in and
through which people constitute identities, simulate belonging,
and pursue freedoms; and endorsement of the difference(s) of
others as a necessary condition for the preservation of one's own
difference. Tolerance of difference alone is not however enough;
support and defence of the difference(s) of others is required.
In short, solidarity has to be constituted amidst and for difference. The unanswered question at the heart of the postmodern
political agenda is how to make common cause to preserve differ-

ences, how to create a sense of solidarity that will be both 'more expansive . . . than we presently have' (Rorty 1989: 196) and conducive to the preservation and enhancement of difference.

NO PLACE LIKE UTOPIA

The present situation is one in which there exists a pervasive and irresistible questioning of the modern institutions, practices, and forms of rationality that have eroded or displaced traditional forms, a thorough-going reflexivity which leaves us with more questions than answers, and in consequence a conviction that modern knowledge does not so much precipitate an accumulation of certitudes as a proliferation of doubts. In brief, more knowledge has not meant less ignorance, for 'the growth of knowledge expands the field of ignorance' (Bauman 1991a: 244). There are, in short, no quick fixes or privileged narratives to which we can turn to resolve the problems and paradoxes we encounter.

If the forms of difference and diversity we encounter are to become something more than simply consequences of marketplace constituted individualised lifestyles; if tolerance is to receive expression communally and solidaristically, rather than through privatised indifference, then it is necessary to envision alternative possibilities, to imagine different ways of coping with and responding to prevailing and future circumstances. In short it is necessary to cultivate 'new political visions, new visions of the body politic' (Levin 1988: 338) which relativise existing social practices and conditions, and thereby open up the prospect, not of the realisation of a social blue-print, a utopian design, but of the possibility of changing things, of transforming prevailing forms of life, for the better.

One conceivable response to such comments is that 'the postmodern political condition is tremendously ill at ease with Utopianism of even a non-Messianic type' (Heller and Feher 1988: 4). And unease concerning utopias is understandable and warranted. But if we are to avoid resigning ourselves to our modern fate it is necessary to reconstitute utopias rather than abandon them (Smart 1992). Bauman's call for 'solidarity' concerning the defence of differences, and all that it implies in terms of a postmodern political agenda and associated articulation of individuals in communities, represents one implicit version. Giddens's identification of the contours of a possible future post-modern order constitutes another, more explicit version. Indeed

Giddens, openly embracing the idea of utopias as necessary to the constitution of preferable 'postmodern' futures, argues that given the counterfactual character of modernity, 'a rigid division between "realistic" and utopian thought is uncalled for' (1990: 155). Hence the promotion of models of 'utopian realism'. This view receives some support from Heller and Feher's observation that the proposal for a 'radicalisation of democracy' deemed necessary for the realisation of appropriate forms of self-determination may appear utopian, but 'the association of Utopian with unfeasibility is completely unjustifiable' (1988: 35).

To alleviate the threat of postmodern conditions and promote the opportunities simultaneously associated with them, to achieve an acceptable and appropriate articulation of forms of diversity with 'communally chosen and communally serviced forms of life' (Bauman 1991a: 273), will certainly require tolerance and solidarity. But imagination will also be required to create the forms of communal life conducive to the preservation and enhancement of diversity. The interrogative character of modern reason, the undermining of answers and displacement of 'solutions' by a radically questioning form of life, simultaneously make necessary the constitution of analytic and existential practices that dare to think and/or imagine the as-yet unthought and the as-yet unexperienced, to imagine the forms of life that might be reflexively constituted through continuing processes of (post)-modernisation. As Rorty remarks, 'human solidarity . . . is to be achieved not by inquiry but by imagination, the imaginative ability to see strange people as fellow sufferers' (1989: xvi). If we are looking for a designation for such practices of the imagination, for the various attempts to exercise upon oneself and others practices which might contribute to the constitution of new forms of thought, new ways of relating to self and others, and hence through the complex reflexive circularity of social life, to new forms of the social, with their own attendant securities and risks, delights and dangers, promises and problems, 'postmodern' seems, for the time being at least, appropriate. In so far as we find ourselves living with, if not at the limits of modernity, modern reason needs to be reconstituted, and to that end perhaps it has become necessary to nourish the *post*modern imagination.

NOTES

[1] See in particular the papers by Alexander; Gordon; Mommsen; Weiss; Albrow; and Roth.

[2] It is appropriate and necessary to note at this point that the standard practice of referring to *the* Enlightenment is problematic. Most analysts and commentators take their bearings from the works of Kant and associated eighteenth-century deliberations on reason. However, Kant's reference is to enlightenment, to a practice, to a particular use of reason which will facilitate people's escape 'from their self-incurred tutelage' (1963: 9). Kant sought to answer the question 'what is Enlightenment?', not to describe or explain *the* Enlightenment (Furbank 1988). The unity implied by the use of the definite article is very much a twentieth-century phenomenon and possibly reflects the increasing prominence of reflections on modernity, itself constituted as a unity, as a distinctive form of life.

5

Heretical discourse

We live in interesting, if rather confusing times. The combination of a sense of new times coupled with an experience of familiar troubles has been described as a typically 'postmodern' phenomenon (Eco 1987). In the postmodern world it seems as though 'past, present, and future coexist in all discourse' (Tyler 1986: 139), a view which receives endorsement in Eco's comments on the continual return of modern ages to the Middle Ages, and to our age as 'neomedieval'. The thawing of the Cold War, the political and economic transformations underway in the societies of formerly existing socialism, the economic and social crises facing the United States of America, the proliferation of ethnic, regional, and infranational struggles threatening (promising) to undermine existing forms of the nation-state, that geopolitical icon of modernity, increasing signs of ecological damage and an associated inability to organise a response at the appropriate global level, the accelerating anti-sociality of cities disintegrating under the impact of excesses of population, communication and transportation, and the various corollaries, for example growing levels of risk, stress, anxiety, uncertainty, terrorism and crime, suggest that we may indeed be living through the transformation of a particularly complex socioeconomic, political and military configuration. Certainly the complacent equation of our age, and Western culture and civilisation and its destiny with an endless modernity has been challenged, if not irrevocably overturned by growing doubts about the feasibility and desirability of the 'project of modernity', and a parallel realisation that accounts with the past, with tradition, have not been settled.

Modernity produces turmoil, flux, and uncertainty, as Marx and Engels tell us in *The Communist Manifesto*. Nothing is sacred and nothing is spared, everything is potentially subject to its subversion, including the 'proletarian' science predicated upon the project of modernity, and more significantly, the claims of modern reason themselves. In short, modernity has become subject to its own critical imperative. The questioning of the project of modernity has been described as part of a process of 'self-clarification of modern thought, as the remnants of tradition and providential outlooks are cleared away' (Giddens 1990: 51). However, I am not convinced that the processes of questioning to which modernity has become subject signify simply a process of self-clarification of modern thought. We now realise that the 'reflexivity of modernity' is antithetical to the gaining of certain knowledge, that under modern conditions our answers are at best provisional, subject to critical reflection and examination, and in due course to doubt, and displacement by further questions. The 'juggernaut of modernity' has indeed left us feeling unsettled, if not confused and disturbed by doubts as certainties crumble beneath our penetrating modern gaze. But does this signify that remaining vestiges of tradition and providential outlooks have been conveniently cleared away? Or is there a sense in which the contemporary interrogation of modernity continues to be articulated with a regeneration or reconstitution of traditional forms of life? The process of questioning to which the project of modernity has been increasingly subject has not, after all, been simply an 'internal' matter; its feasibility and desirability have been questioned and challenged both from within and without.

Undoubtedly the globalisation of modernity has pluralised both social institutions and plausibility structures, multiplied the scope for choice and simultaneously reduced what is received and experienced as destiny or fate. It has also precipitated a universalisation of the heretical imperative. In other words 'as modernization has become a worldwide phenomenon no longer

restricted to its Western matrix, the confrontation with the heretical imperative has also become worldwide' (Berger 1980: 28).
The confrontation identified here is between, on the one hand,
traditional religious practices and understandings, and associated
forms of life, and on the other hand the powerful secularising
process of modernisation, a process which opens up more and
more areas of human existence to the idea and the reality of
choice, and as a corollary, to instability, unreliability, and
anxiety. Under such modern conditions an experience of uncertainty has become widespread, an experience shared by

> the proverbial man in the street and . . . the intellectual
> who spins out elaborate theories about the universe. The
> built-in uncertainty is common to both . . . This basic
> sociological insight is crucial for an understanding of the
> competition between worldviews and the resultant crisis
> of belief that has been characteristic of modernity.
>
> (Berger 1980: 17–18)

Hence the description advanced by Berger of modernity as a
'great relativising caldron'.

The 'vertigo of relativity' implied here is not however a
consequence of modernity alone. The uncertainties and insecurit-
ies we currently encounter are a consequence of the complex
and problematic articulation of the accelerating process of questioning introduced with the project of modernity, and to which
it itself is now subject, and the continuing presence, if not
resurgence, of tradition, providential outlooks, and associated
'inescapabilities and particularities of places, characters, historical trajectories and fates' (Rabinow 1986: 258). The *angst* we
experience is a result of the complex multi-faceted confrontations
which have arisen as the globalisation of a self-questioning and
self-consuming modernity has encountered a resurgence and re-
affirmation of a complex plurality of traditional beliefs and
experiences, or perhaps more appropriately, an affirmation of
traditions anew (Berger 1980: 62). Signs of the latter are evident,
in one important respect at least, in the resurgence of religious
belief and expression, in particular in the effusion of forms of
monotheistic fundamentalism (Sacks 1991).

Undoubtedly there has been some movement from fate to
choice with the advent of modernity. But if the scope for choice
in respect of courses of action, ways of thinking, belief systems,
and the constitution of forms of subjectivity has increased, the

conditions under, or in which choices are exercised, and the range of alternatives available, continue to be substantially and inescapably beyond our choosing. Our modern fate is to be abroad in a world which refuses to submit to both grand and not-so-grand designs, a world which will not accede or accommodate to the ordering programmatic potential of reason, and which disavows the securities of certitude. The contemporary world is one in which an extended scope for choice in respect of conduct and action is continually undermined by the problems of both the unintended consequences of action and the insurmountable reflexivity of social life. The price to be paid for the promise and reality of increasing choice it seems is uncertainty, hesitation, and anxiety, not to mention confrontations with remaining vestiges of tradition, and those forms of tradition (re)constituted anew.

It is to a brief exploration of some of the anxieties and confrontations occasioned by the submission of modernity to its own heretical imperative, and signs of a parallel resurgence and re-affirmation of traditional forms of life, that my discussion here is in part directed.

HERESY AND MODERNITY

Reflecting on the problems of a rational orientation to the world Weber commented that the old gods deprived of their magic would again 'ascend from their graves . . . strive to gain power over our lives and . . . resume their eternal struggle with one another' (1970: 149). A number of recent events, for example the burning of works of fiction, bombing and picketing of cinemas, abrupt withdrawal of corporate promotional material and a television advertising campaign, and publicly expressed condemnation of particular writers, film makers, and performers, including in an extreme case the issuing of a death sentence on an author, lend a degree of credence to such a view. *The Satanic Verses* (Rushdie 1988) has been burnt and criticised, but not necessarily read, by Muslims around the world; performances of *The Last Temptation of Christ* have been interrupted by demonstrations, damage to cinema screens, theft of copies of the film, and bomb incidents; and an advertising campaign for a global beverage, Pepsi-Cola, based on a video of a popular song, *Like a Prayer*, has been withdrawn because scenes depicting the figure of Christ receiving physical comfort and pleasure, possibly even release, from the other Madonna were considered offensive.

The Satanic Verses has been described by Said (1989) as a deliberately transgressive or heretical work, carried out with 'post-modern daring'. Received by Moslems as irreverent, blasphemous and unsympathetic, the text has been condemned for its representation of Islam in terms of terrorism and fundamentalism. The text and its mixed reception illustrate the extent to which the consequences of the articulation of an accelerating process of cultural globalisation with more local or regional constituencies, the particularities of spaces and places, and the peculiarities of different systems of belief are complex, unpredictable, and potentially conflictual (Mazrui 1990). These circumstances have prompted one observer to comment that 'as the world continues to shrink into a global technological village' (Ahmed 1990) the scope for friction between people is likely to increase.

It seems that the contemporary world is one in which we are fated to experience complicated mixtures, for 'there is no pure, unsullied, unmixed essence to which some of us can return, whether that essence is pure Islam, pure Christianity, pure Judaism or Easternism, Americanism, Westernism' (Said 1989). The tone of the responses provoked by what Said calls 'Rushdie's "complicated mixture" ' is paralleled to an extent by comments emanating from the Catholic Church on the subject of two works of fiction by Umberto Eco, *The Name of the Rose* (1984) and *Foucault's Pendulum* (1989). Pope John Paul, described by one commentator as the spiritual twin of the late Ayatollah Khomeini, apparently viewed a video-film of *The Name of the Rose*, heard 'grave' reports of Eco's following book, *Foucault's Pendulum*, and on that basis denounced the author a 'nihilist' (Hebblethwaite 1989). I suspect that this papal pronouncement was meant as a damning criticism, but in a context where the Italian postmodern philosopher Gianni Vattimo (1988) has been advocating the virtues of a stance of 'accomplished nihilism' as more appropriate for contemporary conditions, it might be argued that there is a degree of ambiguity, scope for doubt, and room for speculation about the judgement.

The outrage directed at Martin Scorsese's film *The Last Temptation of Christ* is reminiscent in some respects to the reception which greeted Jean-Luc Godard's film *Hail Mary*, on the subject of the Virgin Mary. Both films offer somewhat unorthodox interpretations of central Christian religious subjects, and in consequence both have been regarded as heretical. In a comparable manner Madonna's provocation of an actor playing the part of Christ in a promotional video, an apparent parody of aspects of Bataille's (1983) transgressive discourse on sexuality in *Story of the Eye*, has constituted an affront to Catholic sensibilities. Each of these discourses may be regarded as heretical in so far as they construct a representation, present a narrative, or espouse a view which departs significantly from prevailing religious beliefs, accepted practices, and orthodox doctrines. In their own idiosyncratic ways they each exemplify the 'diabolical seduction of images' described by Jean Baudrillard (1988a) in *The Evil Demon of Images*. One implication of which is that in an age both blessed and burdened with a proliferating range of global communications technologies, the facility with which cultural boundaries may be crossed increases, as do the potential risks of offence, disagreement and conflict frequently associated with heresy and transgression.

I am not trying to insinuate that such conflictual incidents are features unique or peculiar to the present; on the contrary, heretical discourses have a long history. And I do not propose to attempt either an archaeology of heretical discourse, or for that matter a genealogy of technologies of inquisition. My interest is not so much in specific heretical discourses, and certainly not with a restriction of heresy to the plane of religion alone. Whilst I am intrigued by the various 'neomedieval' manifestations noted above I am more concerned to explore the tendency towards a universalisation of the heretical imperative associated with modernity, and the implications of the idea of emerging postmodern conditions for the possibility of transgression, heresy and critique.

Whilst we are living in what might be termed the modern world, a world shaped by the abstractions of a capitalist market, complex and powerful technological forces of production, bureaucratic forms of organisation and centralised state apparatuses, and increasing concentrations of populations in large metropolitan centres or 'cosmopolitan' cities, there remain vestiges of traditional pre-modern orders or worlds, and more controversially signs of emerging postmodern forms of life. The primary orientation may remain 'this-worldly', secular, and directed towards a realisation of the modern project, yet it is evident that there are substantial, possibly increasing constituencies of people for whom a sacred, 'other-worldly' orientation

continues to be of fundamental significance. If the latter constituencies have resisted or rejected the process of questioning inaugurated by a secularising modern project it has been through a
re-affirmation of commitment and faith, and as a corollary, a
subjection of the project of modernity itself to interrogation. In
a parallel yet significantly different manner, there are other, let
us call them 'postmodern' constituencies, for whom modern
forms of life are no less problematic, but in this instance it is
because 'it has become increasingly difficult, if not impossible at
certain moments, to make sense of our affective experiences
and to put any faith in our [modern] ideological constructions'
(Grossberg 1988: 39). For the latter constituencies commitment,
meaning, and critique now lack a secure foundation or warrant.
In such a context where foundations have been eroded, ortho-
doxes overturned, certainties undermined, and truths relativised,
what are the prospects for heretical discourse, for transgression
and critique?

Our ostensibly solid modern answers do indeed seem to
have melted into air, but I am not convinced that our current
controversies should simply 'be seen as the first real initiatives
in the ambitious task of charting the cultural universe resulting
from the ever-more complete disintegration of the traditional
world' (Giddens 1987: 28–9). It may be difficult to contest the
view that modernity brings with it 'a weakening of every conceivable belief and value . . . [that] modern societies are characterised by unstable, incohesive, unreliable plausibility structures
[and that] in the modern situation certainty is hard to come
by' (Berger 1980: 17). However, the response to a process of
rationalisation which weakens beliefs and values may not be
submission, but re-affirmation, regeneration and reconstitution.
The modern inquisition may be met with resistance, even rejection, rather than compliance.

The steady dismantling of the socio-cultural, political, economic and military rigidities associated with the rhetoric and
reality of the Cold War has been celebrated by some analysts as
a sign that 'West' is indeed best, that capitalism and liberal-
democracy have won (Fukuyama 1989). Another 'end of history'
thesis in fact. However, the process of critical questioning to
which Western civilisation and the project of modernity have
been subject since the turn of the century has not abated; if
anything it is gathering momentum. The transformation of the
post-second world war settlement, the associated problem of a

potential international power vacuum, deepening economic and ecological crises, and the infiltration of 'new faiths and new perspectives of life' (Eco 1987: 74) into the social and cultural body, constitute symptoms of a growing crisis of Western modernity. It is evidence of such transformations that has caused some analysts to speculate about the development of a condition of postmodernity embodied in new cultural and political forms, intellectual practices, and experiences of space and time (Jameson 1984; Aronowitz 1987/1988; Bauman 1987; Harvey 1989).

As one analyst has commented, the deconstruction of developmental history leaves us uncertain about 'which *kinds* of charisma and rationalisation will shape the "postmodern" world' (Roth 1987: 89). Another response to the wide-ranging transformations underway has been to suggest that a reconsideration of the Middle Ages can help us develop an understanding of current conditions and circumstances. A series of developments, for example the growth of homogeneous urban micro-societies; the emergence of 'theaters of permanent tension' and increases in insecurity; deterioration of city life; problems precipitated by technological 'progress'; and dangers associated with travel, lead Eco to conclude that we are experiencing a return of the Middle Ages. He considers in effect that we are living in 'an age of "permanent transition" ', one in which the proliferation of dissidents and heresiarchs constitutes an 'index of a society where new forces are seeking new images of collective life' (Eco 1987: 81), and where older, more traditional forces are re-emerging, reconstituting themselves and their communities anew as they encounter, accommodate to, and in some cases seek to reverse radically transformed conditions and circumstances.

A central feature of the modern condition has been the existence of a multiplicity of possible courses of action, forms of thought, and ways of living potentially available to people. The presence of a diverse range of institutions, lifestyles, world-views or systems of belief means that the modern world is experienced as plural and fragmented, simultaneously emancipatory and alienating, promising and in good part providing new freedoms and potentialities, new forms of self-actualisation and development, along with new problems and difficulties, such as heightened levels of stress and uncertainty, as well as an increasing sense of isolation and loneliness. To the extent that they are unaffected by the relativising forces of modernisation, traditional beliefs and certainties are only rarely subjected to question through heretical deviations in pre-modern forms of life. In contrast modern forms of life are riddled with uncertainty as questioning and 'choosing becomes an imperative' (Berger 1980: 25). The extension of the process of questioning, of 'picking and choosing', to modernity itself has been identified as symptomatic of a radicalisation of modernity (Giddens 1990), or perhaps as representing the emergence of postmodernity. Rather than regard the latter as signifying a break with, or from modernity, I am inclined to follow Lyotard's line, that is to conceive of the postmodern as 'undoubtedly a part of the modern'. Its contribution or significance is to question or suspect '[a]ll that has been received, if only yesterday' (1986: 79). In consequence the postmodern does not so much signal the end of the modern, but rather the pursuit of 'new rules of the game'.

Postmodernity offers us the possibility of a critical view of modernity. Not the end of modernity, but the possibility of a reconstituted modernity. Calling modernity to account, demanding that the costs as well as the benefits are acknowledged, the unintended consequences and the limits recognised, postmodernity re-presents modernity. In a sense it constitutes a taking stock, an owning up, a realisation that some things are not to be and, simultaneously, that others may well be inescapable or unavoidable. Postmodernity represents, as Bauman succinctly summarises it, 'modernity coming of age' (1991a: 272).

REGIMES OF TRUTH AND CRITICISM

Central to our understanding of the modernisation of the West has been a process of secularisation which has, it is said, systematically devalued 'religious institutions, beliefs and practices, substituting for them those of reason and science' (Kumar 1988: 21). But it is increasingly clear that if sacred or religious elements and traditional forms of life have been devalued or displaced they have not disappeared, but rather they have been at most marginalised, concealed or occluded by the 'relativising forces of modernisation' (Berger 1980: 61). Furthermore, as modernity itself has become subject to the relativising forces it initiated, it has become apparent that one of the central problems confronting modernity is an 'inability . . . to deal with "archaic" cultural forms that it somehow sees as being prior to itself – even though they are not' (Bhaba and Parekh 1989: 25). As I have suggested above these forms 'return to question the authority of modernity and reveal its unresolved assumptions' (Bhaba and Parekh 1989: 25–6).

Although modernity has clearly pluralised both institutions and plausibility structures it is evident that a particular rationale of the world has achieved prominence, that the 'charisma of reason' has predominated. To be more precise, in societies such as ours truth is 'centred on the form of scientific discourse and the institutions which produce it' (Foucault 1980: 131), and to a substantial degree all forms of discourse lie in its shadow and remain subject to its measure. But the 'truth' of our (Western) societies is not reducible to scientific rationality alone. The post-Enlightenment world-view evokes particular notions of the individual, material interests, rights and responsibilities, as well as other 'universal' goals and values which are being challenged by a complex combination of reconstituted traditional forms of life and 'postmodern' reflections on both persisting and emerging forms of cultural difference and diversity. One consequence of this is that in a global context it might be argued that 'modernity has become just one element in a mix of historical forces. Tradition and modernity are being amalgamated in various ways that open new directions of rationalisation' (Roth 1987: 89). It is the diversity of forms of life that are emerging from the complex and unpredictable articulations, accommodations and conflicts between tradition and modernity that have been identified as exemplifications of the pluralism and difference(s) constitutive of the 'postmodern world'.

If prophets and priests have to a degree been displaced by scientists and legislators it is increasingly clear that modernity has not had it all its own way, for the progressivist, post-Enlightenment world-view has become more and more contentious as its reach has become global. The questioning of universals, of grounds, foundations, and values, and the corollary, a recognition of cultural pluralism and fragmentation, of diversity and difference are widely acknowledged to be prominent features of the complex contemporary conditions we encounter. More and more we find ourselves living

in a world with an increasing multiplicity of different disciplines and types of knowledge . . . a world of differing ethical standards and social objectives, in which a certain social pluralism is the only answer to either perpetual strife or the tyrannical imposition of one set of

values. At both levels a degree of acceptance of
diversity . . . is necessary.

(Hirst 1990: 21)

As is a sociology committed to the task of interpretation and
translation (Bauman 1988a). However, the turn to interpretation
transforms or recasts, rather than resolves our analytic difficulties. We may have evaded some of the political and analytical
burdens or deficiencies of legislative forms of sociology preoccupied with (i) attempting to adjudicate between competing
accounts of the human condition; (ii) laying claim to supply
truths about the concealed or 'unconscious' dynamics of human
conduct; and (iii) presenting its stocks of knowledge as a sound
basis upon which to generate effective social technologies appropriate for engineering 'conditions that would secure predictable,
patterned human behaviour' (Bauman 1990a: 419), but the alternative, interpretive strategy is itself not free of political and
analytical difficulties. Specifically the difficulties which follow
from the necessary admission that no guarantees can now be
given for either our analyses or our political projects.

Does an endorsement of the interpretive strategy consign us
to the proverbial fence as anxious prophets and restless legislators contend? Must we be resigned to indifference if we rule
out legislative reason? Are we facing a situation in which there
is no longer any ' "reality" with respect to which theory could
become dissident or heretical' (Baudrillard 1987: 125)? Is there
any scope for profanation 'in a world which no longer recognises
any positive meaning in the sacred' (Foucault 1977a: 30)? Given
that 'the "collective security" arrangements of intellectual work
[are] in disarray' (Bauman 1990a: 431), is it the case that 'anything goes' (Feyerabend 1975)? Such 'strange, wicked, questionable questions' betray the continuing powerful influence on contemporary analyses of Nietzsche's (1978: 15) controversial
reflections on (post)modern conditions. But that should occasion
no surprise, for after all it has been suggested that 'philosophical
postmodernity' begins with Nietzsche's work (Vattimo 1988). The
presence of a degree of disorder in the field of intellectual work
is, as we know, by no means a characteristic peculiar to the
present time.

The prospect, if not reality of disarray, is clearly implied in
Nietzsche's late nineteenth-century observation that the faith that
'must always be there first of all, so that science can acquire

from it a direction, a meaning, a limit, a method, a *right* to exist' (1969: 151–2) has been undermined. Science no longer appears self-reliant. Henceforth it requires justification, for the value of science, along with the 'will to truth' on which it is predicated, has been 'called into question' (Nietzsche 1969: 153). Similar sentiments are echoed by Weber (1970) who argues that science is founded on a number of potentially problematic presuppositions concerning the validity and appropriateness of rules of logic and method, and the value of scientific truth. The question of the value of scientific work cannot be finally resolved; rather it is destined to remain open to interpretation and debate in the light of 'our ultimate position towards life' (Weber 1970: 143). It is accumulating reservations of this order, compounded by the increasing erosion of legitimatory grand narratives, that have contributed to the diagnosis of a postmodern condition of knowledge.

Central to the postmodern condition is the notion that the legitimation procedures of knowledge have been eroded, and that the assumption at the heart of legislative reason of the possibility and/or acceptability of deriving prescriptions from denotative statements is no longer sustainable. As Lyotard remarks, 'an important current of postmodernity [is that] science plays its own game; it is incapable of legitimating the other language games. The game of prescription, for example, escapes it. But above all, it is incapable of legitimating itself' (1986: 40). This leaves us with a potential difficulty, namely that in challenging legislative reason and the associated idea that thought develops through a process of progressive enlightenment, or proceeds via a process of overcoming, critical analysis can make no appeal to a more complete foundation. In brief, adoption of critical distance from the notion of an epistemological guarantee, or foundation, as both a resource for and central feature of modern Western thought, leaves us 'unable to criticise Western thought in the name of another, and truer, foundation' (Vattimo 1988: 2).

A comparable conclusion emerges from Rorty's discussion of the differences between 'systematic', scientific, representational discourse and hermeneutic, or 'edifying' discourse. The idea that the former has a 'privileged attachment to reality which makes it *more* than just a further set of descriptions' (Rorty 1979: 361) is considered to be an absurdity, a potentially dangerous form of deception of both self and others. In contrast, an edifying discourse is presented as one which acknowledges the existence of a plurality of discourses, is suspicious of the 'pretensions of epistemology', or sceptical 'about the whole project of universal commensuration' (1979: 366, 368), and which aims not at the constitution of truths which serve to objectify human beings, but at the generation of new descriptions, and different connections between cultures or historical periods, the point being to break 'the crust of convention' (1979: 379). However, 'edifying' discourse has not displaced 'systematic' discourse, any more than a sociology predicated upon 'interpretive' reason has replaced one based upon 'legislative' reason, or 'postmodern' narrative has superseded 'modern' forms of inquiry. In each instance a relationship of difference exists between the respective forms of analysis, a relationship which, in the force field of the social, is manifested as a tension, if not an antagonism, between the claims of 'orthodoxy' and the challenges of 'heresy' (Bauman 1990a).

We find ourselves living amidst a plurality of doctrines and styles of reasoning, but the experience of radical difference is not peculiar to the modern world. A radical incompatibility of ideas, beliefs and institutions seems to have been a feature of the seventeenth century. The difference today, as Hirst makes clear,

> is not that of a plurality of incompatible views, but rather that our incompatible views are about quite different things, such as economic policy or lifestyle politics, and that where differences about religion remain they are in an entirely new context . . .
> A plurality of religious beliefs mattered in the seventeenth century because religion remained the predominant human concern. Today the situation is more complicated. We have multiple domains in which there are pluralities of view, and it is difficult either to rank or to separate them.
>
> (1990: 16)

The new context in which differences are constituted and experienced is a product of a 'complex dialectics of change at both local and global poles' (Giddens 1990: 177), one element of which is the increasing institutionalisation of doubt associated with modernity, another the signs of a significant revival of interest in religious belief evident in the regeneration of various forms of fundamentalism (Sacks 1991).

SIMULATING HERESY

Heresy requires the presence of at least a semblance of orthodoxy, a remaining vestige of an established paradigm, a doctrine
or truth open to contradiction or challenge. Likewise transgression needs a limit, indeed each term evokes the other, for
'a limit could not exist if it were absolutely uncrossable and,
reciprocally, transgression would be pointless if it merely crossed
a limit composed of illusions and shadows' (Foucault 1977a: 34).
In turn critical analysis depends for its challenge upon the existence of a 'regime of truth'.

An address of questions of heresy, transgression, and critique
under conditions of 'post' or 'radical' modernity cannot convincingly avoid a brief acknowledgement of the evil demon of contemporary social theory, and once in play in the text who knows
where Baudrillard's provocations will carry us. There are a
number of inter-related themes running through Baudrillard's
works: the impact of new communications media on culture,
production, and politics; the limitations of Marxist analyses for
understanding post-industrial capitalism; and theoretical reflections on questions of representation, explanation, and analysis.
It is in the context of controversial comments on the latter, on
the dissolution of conventional distinctions between concepts and
objects, representations and realities, and theory and the real,
that Baudrillard's work engages with some of the concerns under
consideration in this chapter.

Baudrillard's work contrives to present a challenge to sociology, Marxism, feminism, psychoanalysis and the work of Foucault, amongst other things. In sum modern social theory is
called into question. Indeed it might be argued that Baudrillard's
work exemplifies a number of the features attributed by Rorty
to a postmodern 'edifying' philosophy. It certainly seems that for
Baudrillard 'the way things are said is more important than the
possession of truths' (Rorty 1979: 359); it may be argued that
his works exemplify a form of ' "poetic" activity' which provides
new aims and ideas requiring us to 'attempt to reinterpret our
familiar surroundings in the unfamiliar terms of our new inventions' (1979: 360); and he quite explicitly endorses the idea that
distinctions between 'theory' and 'the real', 'analysis' and 'world',
have become problematic, and may no longer be theorised in
terms of relations of 'representation' and 'correspondence' (1979:
371–2). It might also be added that, like 'edifying' philosophy,

Baudrillard's discourse is 'parasitic upon normal discourse', epistemology, and the cultural materials of everyday life (Rorty 1979: 365–6). But how could it be otherwise, given that the designated aim of theory and analysis for Baudrillard is to mount a challenge to the real?

The conventional or orthodox modern assumption of the possibility of an exchange between theory and reality is not shared by Baudrillard, who proceeds to argue that the 'real is not an objective status of things', but rather 'the point at which theory can do nothing', in brief, 'the insurmountable limit of theory' (1987: 125). Baudrillard's narrative tends to leave the reader feeling bewitched, bothered and bewildered. His narrative is about a world of simulations, a world in which distinctions and differences between 'realities' and 'referents' have been effaced, a world which is said to be 'hardly compatible with the concept of the real which we impose upon it' (Baudrillard 1988d: 97–8). With the advent of post-industrial (third-order) forms of simulation – by which Baudrillard does not mean illusions of realities but rather 'models of a real without origin or reality: a hyperreal' – differences between concepts or representations and realities dissolve. The real increasingly becomes not so much what can be reproduced as

> *that which is always already reproduced*. The hyperreal . . . Today it is a quotidian reality in its entirety – political, social, historical and economic – that from now on incorporates the simulatory dimension of hyperrealism. We live everywhere already in an 'esthetic' hallucination of reality
>
> (Baudrillard 1983a: 146, 147–8)

And given the above it is argued that the place and contribution of theory must change. There is no longer in Baudrillard's view any ' "reality" with respect to which theory could become dissident or heretical' (1987: 125). In brief, theory can no longer be reconciled with the real, cannot be the reflection of the real, or 'enter into a relation of critical negativity with the real' (Baudrillard 1988d: 97). What remains is for theory to 'defy the world to be more', to challenge the real. After we have made appropriate adjustments for provocative remarks and exaggerated statements, and have noted the presence of apparent contradictions between pronouncements about the end of the real and the impression conveyed by the work that it is 'absorbed by the mystery of correspondences between discourse and the world' (Morris 1988: 191), an impression which receives confirmation in what appear to be *realist* comparisons offered by Baudrillard (1988c) on the subject of modernity in Europe and America, with what are we left? If we concur with Baudrillard then we might conclude, not a lot, for as he admits in an interview, '[t]here is nothing to be had from it' (1987: 135). However, as I have implied, Baudrillard continually overplays his hand and there is no obligation to simulate his fatal flaws.

Baudrillard's questioning of the notion of reality, a 'real world', made accessible by theory and analysis is open to a number of interpretations. I take it to be a challenge to analyses that employ conceptions of 'latent', 'hidden' or 'deep' structures, analyses which effectively assume the possibility of a virtually unmediated access to knowledge of the reality of the world. In contrast Baudrillard suggests that there is no way around, through, or beyond the manifest, the surface. In other words that there is no depth to discover, and that self-referentiality is a feature not only of language, but also increasingly of the culture of (post)modern everyday life. Baudrillard's comments that we now realise that we cannot 'fix the way things are going' (1987: 127); that there 'is no more system of reference'; '[n]othing happens in the real' (1987: 126); and finally that 'it's the objectivity of things we must question' (1987: 125), are exceptionally vague and license a number of possible readings. Related ideas about an unavoidable lack of correspondence between programmes, practices, and their effects, in the real, have been cogently outlined elsewhere (Weber 1970; Foucault 1977b; Giddens 1990). As has the notion that in a cultural setting increasingly subject to the relays of telecommunications, reality 'is always already made by other messages' (Eco 1978: 79). But the key issue, or problem, to which Baudrillard's comments on theory and the real point, for me, is the necessary 'reflexivity or circularity of social knowledge' (Giddens 1990: 153), that is why there seems to be such a 'fatal and enigmatic bias in the order of things' (Baudrillard 1990: 191).

Our theories and analyses of modern social life are unavoidably parasitical upon the understandings of agents in everyday life, they represent constructs of constructs, or interpretations of interpretations, hence the centrality accorded within sociological analysis to what has been described as the 'double hermeneutic' (Giddens 1984). In turn it follows that our knowledge, our theories and analyses of the social world, do not so much reveal features of an independent objectivity as contribute, in both direct and indirect ways, to ongoing complex processes of trans-formation – processes of constitution and re-constitution. Circula-ting ' "in and out" of what it is that they are about' (Giddens 1990: 43), the practices of social theorising and analysis have a transformative effect, and to that extent constitute a critical chal-lenge to the real. Challenging the present institutional 'regime of the production of truth' (Foucault 1980), the certainties through and in terms of which we constitute our social existence and live our lives, continues, to be a feature of contemporary social theory and analysis. Indeed it is at the centre of the debate over postmodern conditions.

I have suggested that heretical discourse is not confined to the domain of religious discourse alone, and that it may be regarded as a core feature of modernity, possibly reaching its apogee under conditions of postmodernity. Indeed if critical 'modern' reactions are anything to go by, the idea of the 'post-modern' would seem to be the very epitome of heresy. The (re)generation of interest in 'postmodern' questions of 'hermen-eutics', 'interpretive reason', and 'edifying' philosophy, alongside and in contrast to 'modern' preoccupations with 'epistemology', 'legislative reason' and 'systematic' philosophy does not signify the end of heresy, transgression, and critique. On the contrary, at least one of the events referred to earlier, and the consequences associated with it, suggest the converse. The debate over *The Satanic Verses* has not only reminded us of the potential impact of the critical written word, but in addition has returned us to a number of difficult questions concerning the interpretation of texts, the responsibilities of writers and intellectuals, and the complex cultural and political problems confronting the (post)-modern world. In particular it has drawn attention, once again, to the potentially volatile relationship between 'sacred' and 'secu-lar' texts. It has also served to remind us of the complex articu-lation of politics and knowledge in a pluralistic global context, of the complex politics of truth we now encounter, and of the difficulty of mediating between 'different cultures, languages and societies . . . the threat of mistranslation, confusion and fear' (Bhaba 1989: 140).

In a series of reflections on responses to *The Satanic Verses* Rushdie (1989) has affirmed the importance of challenging the orthodoxies to which our lives are subject. But if his view that everything 'we know is pervaded by doubt and not by certainty' is endorsed, it is simultaneously necessary to remind ourselves that we 'also face the necessity of imposing justified limits on belief in both the intellectual and the social spheres if the world of knowledge and society . . . is not to be torn apart by the consequences of certain beliefs' (Hirst 1990: 21). We may agree that a radicalised modernity has left us facing questions 'where once there appeared to be answers' (Giddens 1990: 49), but we cannot allow matters to rest there. We need answers, even if they are justifiably recognised to have a relatively provisional, conditional, and even at times contentious status. Likewise we need to be able to differentiate between acceptable and unacceptable practices and positions, the appropriate and the inappropriate, the justified and the 'unjustifiable, invalid, and harmful' (Hirst 1990: 19). And we have to do so in a context where there are no epistemological or political guarantees to which we can appeal.

It is evident that we are living through a period of considerable transformation, a period in which we seem increasingly to be encountering the complex consequences of an accelerating process of globalisation and parallel, in many respects related, difficulties associated with the (re-)emergence of a multiplicity of local identities and affinities. And we appear to be confused by the strange brew of re-affirmed and newly constituted traditions articulated with manifestations of a globally extended modernity, a form of life which itself is increasingly subject to question and criticism, to doubt and challenge. Our world is one of 'criss crossed economies, intersecting systems of meaning, and fragmented identities. Suddenly the comforting modern imagery of nation-states and national languages, of coherent communities and consistent subjectivities, of dominant centers and distant margins no longer seems adequate' (Rouse 1991: 8). Hence the calls for a new 'cognitive mapping' (Jameson 1988), or a new narrative for a 'logically self-contained social condition defined by *distinctive features of its own*' (Bauman 1992: 188); and the numerous related references to 'new times' (Therborn 1989; Hebdige 1989; McRobbie 1991), and to a late, disorganised, flexible-accumulation, neo-Fordist, or post-industrial form of capitalism; the identification of an accelerating process of globalisation and an associated (re-)structuration of the world (Robertson 1990); and the explanation of many of these manifestations in terms of a complex articulation of continuing processes of modernisation with developing forms of *post*modernisation (Lash 1990). Observations such as these and the events and processes to which they refer suggest that we have indeed

> entered a phase . . . of great global uncertainty – so much so that the very idea of uncertainty promises to become globally institutionalised. Or, to put it in a very different way, there is an eerie relationship between the ideas of postmodernism and postmodernity and the day-by-day geopolitical 'earthquakes' which we (the virtually *global* we) have recently experienced.
>
> (Robertson 1990: 16)

It is an existential and analytical uncertainty which arises from complex, overlapping global relationships in which manifestations of simularity exist amidst continuing and newly emerging forms of difference; signs of homogenisation are identified alongside evidence of heterogenisation; and the possibility of forms of convergence and integration are countered by the realities of indigenisation and 'fundamental disjunctures between economy, culture and politics' (Appadurai 1990: 296). It is in this context that heresy has become virtually a universal condition and that plausibility structures have become increasingly particularistic and open to challenge.

Living amidst such a world of difference it is necessary to nurture the conditions conducive to a tolerant and pluralistic social order. But the absence of assured epistemological and political foundations to which we can appeal means that the task of determining the appropriate conditions is destined to remain contentious and incomplete. Living with that prospect is part of the postmodern condition.

6

Global conditions and controversies

In his influential report *The Postmodern Condition* Lyotard suggests that:

> [a] transition has been under way since at least the end of the 1950s, which for Europe marks the completion of reconstruction. The pace is faster or slower depending on the country, and within countries it varies according to the sector of activity: the general situation is one of temporal disjunction which makes sketching an overview difficult.
>
> (1986: 3)

Difficult, but evidently not impossible, for Lyotard proceeds to argue that complex inter-related transformations in social and cultural life, economic activity and technology have had a significant impact upon the 'status of knowledge'. The inquiry conducted by Lyotard is concerned primarily with the ways in which science, research practice and the production and transmission of knowledge are being transformed as a consequence of the 'computerization of society', the 'mercantilization of knowledge', and an associated 'internal erosion of the legitimacy principle of

knowledge' (1986: 39). The brief conclusion frequently drawn
from Lyotard's report is that it is no longer credible to legitimate
knowledge through a metadiscourse which invokes 'some grand
narrative, such as the dialectics of spirit, the hermeneutics of
meaning, the emancipation of the rational or working subject'
(1986: xxiii). And it is the existence of a substantial degree of
'incredulity' towards the metadiscourses which have legitimated
modern science that is identified by Lyotard as definitive of the
postmodern condition of knowledge.

The condition identified describes the state of knowledge,
culture, science, literature, and the arts in the 'most highly
developed societies', by implication the societies of the West.
But the diagnosis implies an emerging more *general* condition,
one that extends beyond knowledge *per se*, one in respect of
which there are variations both between and within countries; a
condition that is articulated with a complex set of developments
that are increasingly effective on a *global* scale. The developments in question, namely the impact of micro-electronic technologies of information, communication and learning, and the accelerating commercialisation of knowledge, as well as the questions
of legitimation they provoke – 'who decides what knowledge is,
and who knows what needs to be decided?' (Lyotard 1986: 9) –
are argued to have far-reaching consequences for the nation-
state and its influence over civil society. The growth of multi-
national corporations and the shift towards more flexible forms
of capital accumulation have already effected a reduction in the
capacity of the nation-state to exercise regulatory control over
economic life. Continuing developments in computer technology
and telematics are exacerbating the situation. As Lyotard
observes,

> The reopening of the world market, a return to vigorous
> economic competition, the breakdown of the hegemony
> of American capitalism, the decline of the socialist alter-
> native, a probable opening of the Chinese market – these
> and many other factors are already . . . preparing States
> for a serious reappraisal of the role they have been
> accustomed to playing since the 1930s.
>
> (1986: 6)

It is not difficult to recognise traces here of themes that are
shared with another narrative, with a contemporary 'grand narrative' constructed around the idea of globalisation. One impli-

cation of this is that postmodernity is a condition closely articulated with processes of globalisation. But given the postmodern is defined in terms of incredulity towards such grand narratives, what are we to make of apparent correspondences between the narratives on globalisation and the condition of postmodernity? When we address the question of postmodernity '[a]re "we" not telling . . . the great narrative of the end of great narratives?' (Lyotard 1988a: 135).

MODERN AGE, WORLD PICTURE

Whether present circumstances are described in terms of the consequences of a process of 'radicalisation' of modernity or the advent of a conduction of postmodernity, there appears to be a mutual identification of the increasing importance of accelerating processes of globalisation. References abound to a global orientation, paradigm, scene, situation, circumstance and arena, not to mention global consciousness, communicative action, civilisation, human condition, economy, political culture and order. Our age does indeed seem to be the 'age of the world picture' (Heidegger 1977). But how do we picture the world? How have we come to conceive of the world as 'a single place with systematic properties' (Robertson and Lechner 1985: 103)? What are the conditions of globalisation? And what are its consequences? It is to an exploration of some aspects of these questions as they bear upon the debate over modern and postmodern conditions that this final chapter is directed.

In a series of reflections on the distinctive characteristics of the modern age Heidegger makes reference to the significance of science, machine technology, the aestheticisation of art, the conceptualisation and consummation of human activity as culture, and the 'loss of the gods'. But what is identified as crucial, as most distinctive about the modern age, is its comprehension of what is as a whole, 'its world picture'. Moreover, the conceptualisation of the world 'in its entirety, is now taken in such a way that it first is in being and only is in being to the extent that it is set up by man, who represents and sets forth' (Heidegger 1977: 129–30). It is in this sense that the modern age is to be distinguished from earlier ages, for it is only with the modern era that 'man becomes subject . . . that being upon which all that is, is grounded as regards the manner of its being and its truth' (1977: 128). This is later described by Foucault as the threshold of our modernity, a threshold 'situated . . . by the constitution of an empirico-transcendental doublet which was called *man*' (1973: 319), an enigmatic reality that is both 'the difficult object and sovereign subject of all possible knowledge' (1973: 310). Or so it has seemed within the modern epistemological configuration in which the human sciences have developed.

One clear implication of the above is that the existence of a conception of the world in its entirety is what distinguishes the modern age from other eras. As Heidegger remarks, in both classical antiquity and the Middle Ages comprehension of that which is, of Being, differs significantly from the modern age. In classical antiquity thought and Being are synonymous, 'the apprehending of whatever is belongs to Being' and in the Middle Ages 'that which is . . . is created by the personal Creator – God' (Heidegger 1977: 130). In both periods whatever is does not stand as object before the figure of 'man'. It is only with the development of the modern epistemological configuration and associated modern forms of representation that the world has become picture. In other words '[t]hat the world becomes picture is one and the same event with the event of man's becoming *subjectum* in the midst of that which is' (Heidegger 1977: 132). A subject which in turn has sought through the modern project to exercise mastery over the world, a familiar theme endorsed in one form by Marx, lamented in another by Weber and criticised in a great many respects by the theorists of the Frankfurt School.

The modern age has been preoccupied with the conquest of the world it has constituted as a structured and systematic unity and in its decisive unfolding 'the modern relationship to that which is . . . becomes . . . a confrontation of world views' (Heidegger 1977: 134). The signs, Heidegger remarks, are 'everywhere and in the most varied forms and disguises', in the appearance of the gigantic and simultaneously 'the tendency toward the increasingly small' as well as 'in the annihilation of great distances by the airplane, [and] in the setting before us of foreign and remote worlds in their everydayness, which is produced at random through radio by a flick of the hand' (1977: 135). Heidegger's concern is to explore what it is that constitutes the 'fundamental event of the modern age', what it is that distinguishes the modern age from earlier eras. But the signs identified might also be regarded as earlier moments, phases or manifestations of continuing processes of transformation now conceptualised in terms of a process of globalisation and a condition of postmodernity.

In so far as it questions the modern age, modern science and technology, and interrogates Western metaphysics, 'the notion of foundation, and of thought both as foundation and means of access to a foundation' (Vattimo 1988: 2), Heidegger's work contributes to and allows us to understand the crises of representation which have beset the arts, literature, philosophy and scientific knowledge, crises which have been identified as symptoms of a postmodern condition (Boyne and Rattansi 1990: 13). It has been suggested that along with the works of Nietzsche the ideas of Heidegger 'offer us the chance to pass from a purely critical and negative description of the post-modern condition, typical of early twentieth century *Kulturkritik* and its more recent offshoots, to an approach that treats it as a positive possibility and opportunity' (Vattimo 1988: 11). What Vattimo has in mind here is that it is now possible to take leave of Western humanism and metaphysics without a deep sense of loss, for a series of transformations have created the conditions in which a 'different possibility of existence . . . emerges' and in consequence the works of Nietzsche and Heidegger 'appear less apocalyptic and more in line with our own experience' (1988: 11). The transformations identified include the dispersion of the mass media 'across the face of the earth' and associated processes of 'simulacrization' and 'commercialization', the impact of computer technology on developed economies and the possibility of a 'new social order based on the diffusion of information systems'. These developments, which Vattimo suggests 'gesture toward a possible new human experience' (1988: 26), are frequently considered to be constitutive features of a process of globalisation.

GLOBAL SOCIOLOGY OR A SOCIOLOGY OF GLOBALISATION?

The question of the impact of processes of globalisation on national traditions, cultures and economies is now acknowledged to be an important focus for sociological inquiry. We may not yet live in a 'single world society' but it is argued that each 'major aspect of social reality . . . is simultaneously undergoing globalisation, as witnessed by the emergence of a world economy, a cosmopolitan culture and international social movements' (Archer 1990: 1). The suggestion is that globalisation is affecting

us all, that in some respect or another our activities, our conditions, what we know of, believe, respond or react to are, to a
variable degree, affected by the international economy; by the
proliferation of global forms of communication; by agencies and
movements operating transnationally to confront issues on a
world scale; by changes in climate induced by patterns of production and consumption, military conflicts and other catas-
trophes; and so forth.

Besides the need to go beyond the equation of society and
nation-state as the focus of sociological inquiry, a response which
has a broad degree of support within the discipline, it is argued
that we cannot continue 'to think and to theorise as once we
did' and further, that identification of worldwide diversity alone
is not sufficient. In consequence the task proposed for sociology
is 'the integration of this diversity'. It is a task which is said to
involve 'the exposing, the juxtaposing and the synthesising of
diversity, which culminates in generating a new variety of social
theory' (Archer 1990: 1). Elaborating on the task Archer refers
to two recent trends that need to be approached with caution,
namely the ' "indigenisation" of sociology' and the 'upsurge of
"post-modernism" '. Both are said to challenge justifiably particular aspects of modernity, in particular the inappropriate universalising of specific models, concepts and frameworks derived
from Western experience. However, the corollary is that 'indigenisation' and 'post-modernism' also threaten to obstruct the
development of a 'genuinely universal' sociology; 'indigenisation'
in so far as it may lead to the generation of 'incommensurable
models which are incommunicable to other parts of the world'
and 'post-modernism' because in so far as it tolerates 'the incommensurable and the inconsistent, it undercuts the tough endeavour of international sociology which is to render different cultures
intelligible to one another' (1990: 2). There are a number of
controversial and complex matters to be considered here.

The stated objective of rendering different cultures intelligible to one another is not of itself problematic. How intelligibility between cultures is to be enhanced, what contribution
sociology is able to make, or perhaps more accurately, what
kind(s) of sociology can make an appropriate contribution, are
rather different and potentially more contentious matters. Whilst
Archer acknowledges the appropriateness of postmodern scepticism about the 'linear spread of modernity' and the modernisation process, no consideration is given to the possibility of

related implications for a sociology 'bound up with the "project of modernity" ' (Giddens 1987: 26). On the contrary, the parallel observation that the integration of diversity 'through progressive sociological dialogue . . . has to be premised upon interlocution between cultures' and that this in turn assumes 'the unicity of human nature and the universality of human reasoning' (Archer 1990: 2) looks very much like a re-affirmation of the conventional wisdoms of modern sociology. In a sense it assumes that which needs to be clarified and explored.

Does interlocution between cultures depend upon commensurability and common ideas about human nature and reason? Or is it that through dialogue cultures come to an appreciation of their differences, their almost indefinable incommensurabilities? Do we want to integrate diversity, or contribute to the growth of tolerance and solidarity between different cultures and communities? The very idea of 'international sociology' or 'global sociology' already seems to assume the existence of a degree of commensurability between cultures, the accommodation of difference or diversity within the same, within a single narrative. And as is well known such a sociological narrative interested in global processes and committed to the identification of universals may be 'traced back at least as far as the Enlightenment' (Featherstone 1990: 3). The critical issue here is the terms on which a sense of commensurability is to be established and difference or diversity are to be accommodated.

The age of the world picture, modernity, is described by Heidegger as an age which is witnessing the 'complete Europeanisation of the earth and man' (1971: 15). Yet if there seems to be no escape from 'modern technicalisation and industrialisation'; no effective alternative but to accept that the language in which dialogue generally occurs is European, that discussion is 'forced over into the sphere of European ideas'; and that there is an almost irresistible temptation to 'rely on European ways of representation and their concepts', a tendency that confirms and lends weight to the 'dominance of . . . European reason', dialogues between cultures remain disturbed and troubled by the sense that the language in which dialogue takes place may prevent 'the possibility of saying what the dialogue is about' (Heidegger 1971: 13–16, 5). In so far as the languages of cultures are not simply different 'but are other in nature and radically so' then interlocution between cultures will continue to be subject to interference, to misunderstandings and misinterpretations, no matter how 'universal' our assumptions might be, or rather, particularly when we *assume* the existence of universality. Indeed it might be argued that under present conditions, the era of global simulations, the difficulties identified by Heidegger and explored further by critics of modernity have increased. European or Western modernity is no longer unchallenged, for there are now a number of contending 'civilisational, continental, regional, societal, and other definitions' of global conditions and possibilities (Robertson and Lechner 1985: 111), other conceptions and images of the wider world. As Lyotard reminds us, 'the great narratives of legitimation that characterise Western modernity . . . are concerned . . . with the "transcendence" of particular cultural identities in favour of a universal civic identity. But how that transcendence takes place is far from obvious' (Benjamin 1989: 321). And given the de-centring or waning of Western modernity in the face of resistance on the part of the 'insurmountable diversity of cultures' (1989: 319), transcendence of particular cultural identities appears to be a much more questionable project and prospect. Indeed with the growth of world markets and multi-national corporations since the end of the second world war cultural differences have remained prominent and have been 'promoted as touristic and cultural commodities at every point on the scale' (Benjamin 1989: 323).

The idea that contemporary sociology needs to extend the focus of its inquiries beyond the forms of social life nurtured within the geopolitical boundaries of the modern nation-state, to encompass transnational and/or global forms of sociality, is well taken. But in contrast to the idea of a 'global sociology', with its connotations of a universalising, indivisible discipline, I prefer the notion of a sociology of globalisation, or better still, sociological analyses of processes of globalisation. The idea of a 'global sociology' implies that there already exists a worldwide culture; it retrieves the notion of 'society' and elevating it to a global level suggests that 'the peoples of the world are incorporated into a single world society, global society' (Albrow 1990: 9), through processes of globalisation. In brief it is the assumed existence of a novel phenomenon 'global society' that is promoted as the rationale for a global sociology. I intend to proceed differently, to focus on sociological conceptions and analyses of processes of globalisation in order to explore the ways in which global transformations have led simultaneously to the dispersion of particular common forms, commodities, and ideas and yet, in so far as these are received and interpreted in quite different cultural contexts, have contributed to the (re)production and (re)constitution of difference and diversity. This does not mean that the aim of rendering different cultures intelligible to one another is rejected. However, as my earlier comments suggest I do not see this as the project of sociology alone. Moreover, if the central objective is to enhance intelligibility between different cultures and we accept that we cannot 'continue to think and to theorise as we once did', it might be argued that a postmodern 'interpretive' sociology, injudiciously dismissed in the haste to promote the prospectus for a growing international profession, is better placed than a modern 'legislative' sociology reconstituted as a global discipline (Bauman 1987, 1988a).

GLOBALISATION: CONCEPTIONS AND ANALYSES

Behind the increasing sociological attention devoted to the question of globalisation is a sense that an adequate understanding of social life, social relations, identity and experience can no longer be derived from an analysis limited in scope to 'society', particularly where the latter is conceptualised as equivalent to the geopolitical order of the modern nation-state. As Touraine has recommended, the classical sociological model of social life needs to be radically amended for its constitutive elements, 'the ideas of modernity and national state and . . . their fusion into the central notion of modern society, are undergoing a process of decomposition' (1984: 37). But if this means it is necessary to break with established ideas about Western modernisation that have been accorded the status of universals it does not follow, for Touraine at least, that we should be speaking of a 'postmodern society' or announcing a 'postmodern era'. Although, as I will try to show, many of the transformations documented may be, indeed have been, identified by other analysts as manifestations or signs of an emerging condition of postmodernity.

The situation described by Touraine is one in which the fragile unity ascribed to national societies has begun to dissolve, to fragment, as transnational and global exchanges and communications have gathered momentum, and infranational differences expressed in the form of 'local, regional and ethnic cultures' (1984: 38) have been reconstituted or regenerated. This does not mean that national societies are destined to disappear for 'the strongest trend still is toward a growing and more centralised capacity of action of national societies upon themselves' (1984: 38). But the shape and identity of existing national societies are being challenged both from within and without, by ethnic and regional expressions of difference and parallel demands for autonomy and independence, as well as by global population movements, transnational communication networks and associated transformations in economic activity, in the production, marketing and patterns of consumption of goods and services. As communities, communications and '[c]ultural products are internationalized, people travel extensively, [and] ideas and goods are exchanged in a much higher proportion than two generations ago' (1984: 39) so the assumption that sociality, identity and meaning are constituted solely within parameters that coincide closely with those of the modern nation-state and its institutional orders becomes unsustainable. This does not mean, however, that the nation-state itself becomes unsustainable, although in a context where, as Bell remarks, it 'has become too small for the big problems in life, and too big for the small problems' (1980: 225) it undoubtedly is in difficulty.

The conclusion to which Touraine is drawn is that in circumstances where the political and legal boundaries of the nation-state coincide less and less with the complex patterns of social life and the persisting if not developing diversity of cultural configurations: (i) 'internal identification with the nation through images and beliefs tends to give way to an external one based on the awareness of international relations of competition and domination' (Touraine 1989: 15); and (ii) Western modernity can no longer be represented as a 'unity' or promoted as the 'universal' in contrast to other worlds. Given these circumstances social analysis has of necessity to adopt a global perspective, to move towards an exploration of processes of global transformation.

Appreciation of the increasing significance of transocietal or global transformations has undoubtedly opened up the analytic 'frame beyond . . . the usual interpretation of concern with "modernity"'' (Robertson and Lechner 1985: 105) and has encouraged conjecture about present conditions. For example, the conditions under which we live have been described, once more, as constituted in the final instance by 'the real world of the capitalist world-economy' (Wallerstein 1990: 47);[1] but also as shaped by 'cultural communities, from the Catholic Church and Islam to secular ideologies and movements . . . which transcend the boundaries of even the largest and most centralised state' (Worsley 1990: 94); and again as revealing traces of post-national, post-industrial and postmodern forms of life (Smith 1990: 175). As Robertson and Lechner observe,

> the problem of modernity has been expanded to – in a sense subsumed by – the problem of globality. Many of the particular themes of modernity – fragmentation of life worlds, structural differentiation, cognitive and moral relativity, widening of experiential scope, ephemerality – have been exacerbated in the process of globalisation.
>
> (1985: 108)

It is the aggravation and diffusion of these themes, coupled with a sense that they constitute intrinsic features rather than pathological aberrations of modernity, that have been diagnosed as symptoms of a condition of postmodernity.

The ideas of globalisation and postmodernity have come to the fore during the twentieth century as the process of modernisation has expanded to take in virtually the whole world. As modernity has achieved a global reach it has become fragmented, and has lost much of its 'vividness, resonance and depth, and . . . its capacity to organise and give meaning to people's lives' (Berman 1985: 17). It is precisely this sense of facing up to the limits and limitations of modernity that is evoked by the idea of postmodernity. To be more precise a condition of postmodernity has been equated with a series of global transitions beginning in the 1960s, transitions associated with information technology, computerisation and the mercantilisation of knowledge (Lyotard 1986); a 'prodigious expansion' and 'fundamental mutation of the sphere of culture in the world of late capitalism' (Jameson 1991: 47–8); and a 'speed-up in the turnover times of capital' achieved through another round of 'time-space compression' (Harvey 1989: 285, 299, 306). These and other global transitions, for example the end of the Cold War and fears concerning the spread of nuclear weapons; 'problems of multiculturality and polyethnicity' confronting modern nation-states; the increasing 'accentuation of "post-materialist" values' (Robertson 1990: 27); and the growth of institutions, movements and networks of communication addressing, invoking or attempting to fabricate global constituencies, have contributed to a pervasive sense of uncertainty, to the condition of postmodernity.

If the world is becoming 'a single place with systematic

properties' (Robertson and Lechner 1985: 103), there nevertheless continue to be a number of different and competing views
of global relations and processes, a range of different ideas about
global system dimensions, their articulation, and consequences.
As a number of analysts emphasise, globalisation is about the
conditions and consequences of global interactions, interactions
that may be economic, financial, technological, cultural, political
and military. The global expansion of capitalist economic activity,
now cultivating markets in Eastern Europe and the Soviet Union,
the development of a truly worldwide economy, and the construction of a global financial system in which 'boundaries between
distinctive functions like banking, brokerage, financial services,
housing finance, consumer credit and the like have become
increasingly porous at the same time as new markets in com-
modity, stock, currency, or debt futures have sprung up' (Harvey
1989: 161) have been well documented (Lash and Urry 1987;
Castells 1989). So too have developments in technology that have
'tied the world together in almost real time' (Bell 1980: 212;
Harvey 1989). The political and military dimensions of globalisation have also been clearly identified. Indeed in respect of the
former it has been argued that just as 'corporations are the
dominant agents within the world-economy' so 'nation-states are
the principal "actors" within the global political order' (Giddens
1990: 71). One of the major manifestations of action on the part
of nation-states which has become potentially global in scope is
the expression of military power. As war has become industrialised, if not in the case of the 1991 conflict in the Persian Gulf,
Kuwait and Iraq 'post-industrialised', and weapons systems have
become technologically more sophisticated, powerful, and,
through the growth of an international arms industry, more
widely available, so the consequences of military conflicts
between nation-states and/or alliances of states have become
increasingly global in scope.

One of the potential military conflicts between an alliance
of nation-states, justifiably recognised to be not simply global in
scope but in all probability terminally so, has diminished significantly with the end of the Cold War. But if an apocalyptic sequel
to the conflicts which commenced in 1914 and 1939, world wars
described by Toynbee (1954b: 422, 467) as 'postmodern', now
appears somewhat less threatening, it is increasingly evident that
the prospect and fear of nuclear war and its global consequences
is not going to go away, particularly given the increasing potential

for a global spread of nuclear weapons and associated technologies. Fears about nuclear proliferation have been exacerbated by the political fragmentation of the Soviet Union. As the union has dissolved and been replaced by a fragile, possibly temporary, Commonwealth of Independent States striving to achieve autonomy from Moscow, so the prospect of an increase in the number of sovereign states possessing nuclear weapons has grown. To the list of nations already known to possess nuclear weapons, that is the USA, a number of republics of the former USSR, France, Great Britain and China, and those often reported to possess such weapons, notably Israel and South Africa, we have to add a list of nations believed to be both in possession of appropriate nuclear technology and on the way to developing weapons systems (e.g. Iraq, Iran, Algeria, North Korea, and Libya). The threat of nuclear proliferation identified by Bell (1980) as one of the sources of a 'future world disorder', seems increasingly to be already upon us.[2]

The dimensions outlined above, namely the world capitalist economy, the nation-state system, the worldwide diffusion of modern technologies and an associated expansion of the division of labour, and the emergence of a 'world military order' are acknowledged to be key features of the process of globalisation (Giddens 1990: 63–77). However, an additional dimension, the cultural dimension of globalisation, has become increasingly prominent and it is to this fundamental dimension that I will direct most of my attention.

Alongside the development of a global economy; the growth of transnational corporations, financial institutions and networks; new communications and information technologies which have contributed to an 'intensification of time-space compression that has had a disorienting and disruptive impact upon political-economic practices' (Harvey 1989: 284); and increases in international travel and the migration of populations, parallel transformations in social and cultural life have been identified. Analysts have made reference to the emergence of a 'cosmopolitan' culture (Archer 1990; Hannerz 1990), to the idea that we are witnessing the formation of 'transnational cultures' (Smith 1990), as well as to the possibility that we might be moving towards a fulfilment of the modern notion of a common humanity through the creation of a 'unitary global culture' (Smith 1990; Tenbruck 1990). Implied in each instance is a series of complex issues concerning: the articulation of global processes with local or regional differences; tensions between processes of 'cultural homogenization and cultural heterogenization' (Appadurai 1990: 295); and a distinction between 'modernist homogenization' on the one hand and 'ethnic and cultural fragmentation' on the other as 'two constitutive trends of global reality' (Friedman 1990: 311).

The idea of a 'global culture' appears in many instances to be the determined superstructural corollary of global economic and technological infrastructures and associated institutional forms. It is an idea that seemingly derives its impetus from the 'new world of economic giants and superpowers, of multinationals and military blocs, of vast communications networks and international division of labour' (Smith 1990: 174). It portrays a world in which the operations of transnational corporations and the effects of telecommunications systems and computerised information networks are interfering with, if not displacing the 'cultural networks of more local units, including nations and ethnic communities' (1990: 175). In brief the suggestion is that we are seeing a shift from ethnic or national cultural imperialisms to 'supranational' forms predicated upon a truly 'cosmopolitan' technological infrastructure, one which 'will eventually erode cultural differences and create a genuinely "global culture" ' (1990: 176). In this context global culture is pictured to be 'eclectic, universal, timeless and technical', literally a simulation of global telecommunications systems, a 'constructed' culture.

The objections outlined by Smith, Tenbruck, Friedman and others to the idea of a global culture are not so much that it is constructed; after all the traditions and cultures associated with nations and ethnic communities may, to a degree, be regarded as inventions or fabrications (Anderson 1983; Hobsbawm and Ranger 1983); they are that it offers little if any account of the ways in which supposedly 'cosmopolitan' cultural forms articulate with and give expression to the identities and circumstances of national, 'local' or 'regional' communities. In contrast to national or ethnic cultures which are 'particular, timebound and expressive' and invoke shared characteristics – feelings, values and memories, a sense of historic identity and a common destiny – 'global and cosmopolitan culture fails to relate to any such historic identity . . . is memoryless . . . [and] answers to no living needs, no identity-in-the-making' (Smith 1990: 179–80). The absence of a common past, shared memories and a collective identity to which it might appeal, and in turn give expression, renders the idea of a global culture both premature and potentially misleading. But the fact that there seems to be relatively little mileage at present in the idea of a global culture does not bring the question of the cultural dimension of globalisation to a close. The relationships between 'transnational' homogenising processes and local 'territorial' forms of cultural diversity need to be explored, as do the complex 'disjunctures between economy, culture and politics' (Appadurai 1990: 296), and the consequences of global communications networks, commodities and imagery for individual cultures.

The question of the articulation of global processes with local practices and customs is a question about the diffusion of the institutions of modernity and their consequences. It has been suggested that the global diffusion of modernity has brought about the 'dissolution' or 'disintegration' of the traditional world and that it is the complex cultural consequences of this process to which the ambiguous and premature notion of postmodernity refers (Giddens 1987). On this issue I am inclined to lean more towards the view that pre-modern traditions, ties and sentiments are still prevalent (Smith 1990); that 'the nation is not only a component of modernity . . . [but in so far as] its interpretive constitution involves a pre-existent ethnic core, it is also a changing combination of tradition and modernity . . . [an expression of the] ongoing reactivation of tradition within modernity' (Arnason 1990: 228–9); and that the corrosive consequences of modernity may, and have been met with a re-affirmation and reconstitution of tradition (Berger 1980). It is important to understand, as Touraine indicates, 'that the modern does not replace the traditional as day replaces night but that tradition is also the source of its own transformation or at least can be reinterpreted' (1989: 30).

It is in this context, one in which cultures communicate, compete, contrast and conflict with one another on a global scale and contribute to an 'intellectual fragmentation of the world' (Friedman 1990: 311) which effectively undermines the claims to universality of any one particular narrative, that a concept of postmodernity may temporarily have a place. Postmodernity not as a 'countermodernity' or a nostalgic recalling of a 'pre-modernity', but perhaps as a way of describing experiences of, relationships to, and struggles with the diverse and complex manifestations of a modernity that is still very much with us.

ORGANISATIONS OF DIVERSITY

Although we live in an increasingly interdependent world, it remains a world 'marked by an organisation of diversity rather than by a replication of uniformity' (Hannerz 1990: 237). A world of differences, of competing cultures and divergent cultural experiences. It is a world in which a plurality of distinctive cultural entities exist, some of which receive articulation in the form of a 'national identity' and achieve embodiment in the institutional form of the nation-state. The proliferation of nation-states and national cultures illustrates that rather than creating the conditions for the constitution of a world society, the globalisation of modernity, through diverse complex articulations with traditional, ethnic and/or folk cultural forms, has effectively contributed to the recasting of cultural differences. As Arnason notes,

> If the structure of modernity lends itself to variations which depend on the historical context, it is by the same token open to a partial determination by the traditional background. The diversity of cultural traditions is thus reflected in the configurations of modernity as well as in the roads to it. This does not mean that the unity which can no longer be guaranteed by an idea or a project of modernity is restored on the level of particular traditions. It is more frequently the case that internal tensions and conflicts of the tradition are reactivated in a new context. And the synthesis of tradition and modernity should be seen as a matrix of further changes, rather than a stable model.
>
> (1990: 221)

In other words the geopolitical institutional form of the modern nation-state may have become global but the processes by which distinctive cultural communities have cultivated or forged a sense of national identity and succeeded in constituting themselves as nation-states have varied considerably, according to what Smith describes as the 'ethno-history' (1990: 181) of each community and what Arnason refers to as the 'different civilisational legacies and corresponding roads to modernity' (1990: 230).

Rediscovered ethno-histories and civilisational legacies are threatening the semblance of unity represented by existing transnational cultures and nation-states that do not correspond with a distinctive ethnic community. For example, both the former USSR and the USA are experiencing differing degrees of difficulty with the dislocating consequences of revalorised ethnohistories and identities. In the USSR the latter effectively led to the deconstruction of the idea of 'Soviet culture' and thereby have contributed to the fragmentation of the union. In the USA the impact of demographic changes (e.g. birth rates; migration) on the pattern of cultural diversity, coupled with the significance of ethno-history for identity formation, has given rise to concern about the disarticulation of American society (Rouse 1991: 16). The implication is not that transnational cultures are necessarily in decline, although that does appear to be the fate of Soviet communism, but that the more interdependent world which has been constituted through processes of globalisation is simultaneously one in which there seems to be an increasing tendency for ethnic communities both to challenge wider polities within which they are incorporated and to pursue the status of modern nationhood. As Smith observes, 'national cultures inspired by rediscovered ethno-histories, continue to divide our world into discrete cultural blocks, which show little sign of harmonisation . . . Feeding on each other, ethnic nationalisms seem set to multiply and accentuate national and ethnic boundaries' (1990: 185). In turn the implied proliferation of national identities and perspectives raises the prospect of different interpretations of and responses to global configurations, '*competing* societal (and other) definitions of the global situation' (Robertson and Lechner 1985: 110).[3]

The rediscovery of ethno-histories and the global diffusion or crystallisation of modern political forms have been identified as contributing to the multiplication of ethnic nationalisms, an enlargement of the actual and potential 'world of nations', and the persistence of diversity. However, other parallel processes and related developments, notably 'the partial mixing of cultures, the rise of lingua franca and of wider "Pan" nationalisms' are considered by Smith to 'have created the possibility of "families of culture" which portend wider regional patchwork culture-areas' (1990: 188). What is acknowledged here is the possibility of cultural configurations that neither correspond to nor displace the cultural constituencies of the ethnic community and the nation, configurations which may be regional or transterritorial but do not correspond to the idea of a global culture. Appropriate examples might be the modern resurgence of Islam which is now 'multinational and widely spread out on the globe' (Mazrui 1990: 224) and the family of cultural assumptions and traditions ('Roman law, Renaissance humanism, Enlightenment rationalism, romanticism, democracy' (Smith 1990: 187)) which constitute a common configuration within and across the national cultures of Europe and provide part of the context for ongoing attempts to construct a more integrated and united Europe out of existing forms of economic, political and military cooperation.

With the global diffusion of modernity cultures have been brought into a network of complex interrelationships. Increasingly we are the decentred subjects of, and find ourselves subject to not simply the cultural unity of a particular ethnic community but, simultaneously, other infranational cultures as well as national, regional, transnational, perhaps even inter-continental cultures. Our identity and conduct are formed by the complex and shifting articulations we encounter, interpret, and respond to between the different levels and orders of culture. In so far as transterritorial or transnational cultural forms cross linguistic and national cultural boundaries it has been argued that the associated diffusion of 'cross-cultural images and messages . . . [leads to] individual cultures . . . losing their autonomy' (Tenbruck 1990: 205). There are two things to be said here. First, although it may be argued that there are convincing signs of transnational cultural forms – 'audiences, movements, issues, images and lifestyles' (1990: 205) – it should not simply be assumed that these signify an inevitable process of cultural homogenisation. As Appadurai cautions, such 'arguments fail to consider . . . that at least as rapidly as forces from various metropolises are brought into new societies they tend to become indigenized in one or other way: this is true of music and housing styles as much as it is true of science and terrorism, spectacles and constitutions' (1990: 295). In short individual cultures may be reproducing or reconstituting their specificity by indigenising transnational cultural forms. In other words we need to be attuned to both 'the global institutionalization of the life-world and the localization of globality' (Robertson 1990: 19).

The second observation to be made on the prospect of individual or national cultures losing their autonomy is that there is little evidence to suggest 'a global diminution of the power of nationalism or the hold of national cultures in the next few decades' (Smith 1990: 185). And yet if national cultures remain pivotal in the organisation of global diversity there are continuing processes of transformation taking place that ought to be noted, transformations that are in substantial part a continuing legacy of the imperialistic expansion of European cultures and the military, technological, political and economic strategies they employed both to constitute themselves as nations and to acquire colonies and empires. The consequences of the modern constitution of nationhood, acquisition and subsequent relinquishment of colonies and empires are still very much with us, and manifest in particular in ongoing struggles, conflicts, and controversies over the preservation, making and/or unmaking of nations; post-colonial relations of dependence and interdependence between nation-states; and the proliferation of migrant communities which contribute to the constitution of transnational cultures and circuits. Tololyan argues that 'the past five centuries have been a time of fragmentation, heterogeneity and unparalleled mass dispersion . . . [and that] migrations have led to a proliferation of diasporas' (1991: 4). In the course of the twentieth century the increasing migration of populations and associated growth of diasporas ('exemplary communities of the transnational movement') in conjunction with the global organisation of economic production and financial networks, growth of transnational corporations, and pervasive global presence of electronic mass media (Tenbruck 1990), have required nation-states to recognise 'the extent to which their boundaries are porous and their ostensible homogeneity a multicultural heterogeneity' (Tololyan 1991: 5). However, infranational and transnational pressures and constituencies do not signal the demise of the nation-state; on the contrary the latter continues to represent a key element in the organisation of global diversity. But whilst the nation-state has remained a privileged form of polity the modern imagery articulated with it ('coherent communities and consistent subjectivities . . . dominant centers and distant margins') seems less convincing and appropriate. As Rouse acknowledges, 'this mobilisation of modern socio-spatial images has become increasingly unable to contain the postmodern complexities it confronts' (1991: 12).

CULTURAL FLOWS AND DISJUNCTURES

The identification of disjunctures between economy, technology, culture and politics has been a feature of analyses of transformations in advanced industrial capitalist societies. For example, in his well known controversial essay on 'the future of advanced industrial societies' in which a number of key developments are identified, including the increasing interdependence of the world economy, the growth of information and telecommunications networks, international travel and global organisations and corporations, Daniel Bell (1973) refers to an increasing disjunction between social structure ('economy, technology and the occupational system'), culture and politics. Bell's objective is to offer a social forecast about a series of developments taking place most prominently at the time in America, transformations identified as manifestations of the possible emergence of 'post-industrial society'. It is speculated by Bell that the consequences of post-industrial forms of social and economic life will, by the end of the century, be particularly evident in the United States, Japan and Western Europe. I do not intend to explore the idea of post-industrial society any further in this context, or for that matter the question of the relationship that might be held to exist with the notion of postmodernity (Smart 1992). It is sufficient for my purposes here to emphasise that Bell's thesis 'that culture, politics, and economy each operate according to their own independent "axial principles", rather than one determining the others' (Block 1990: 7) has been regarded as an important contribution to the antideterminist orientation prominent within contemporary social theory. It is precisely this kind of antideterminist orientation that Appadurai (1990) brings to bear on the question of 'the new global cultural economy' and associated disjunctures between economy, culture and politics.

Rather than assume a singular process of globalisation Appadurai presents an analysis in which growing disjunctures between a series of key global dimensions are said to give rise to diverse, increasingly fluid and hence unpredictable global conditions and flows. The dimensions of global cultural flow differentiated – ethnoscapes; technoscapes; finanscapes; mediascapes; and ideoscapes – parallel those already discussed above. However, by emphasising that these constructs are 'deeply perspectival' Appadurai reminds us that there is no longer an unchallenged foundation, metanarrative or objective reference point for understanding social relations and social processes. On the contrary, observations are

> inflected very much by the historical, linguistic and political situatedness of different sorts of actors: nation-states,

multinationals, diasporic communities, as well as sub-national groupings and movements (whether religious, political or economic), and even intimate face-to-face groups, such as villages, neighbourhoods and families. Indeed, the individual actor is the last locus of this perspectival set of landscapes . . . These landscapes . . . are the building blocks of . . . 'imagined worlds', that is, the multiple worlds which are constituted by the historically situated imaginations of persons and groups spread around the globe.

(Appadurai 1990: 296–7)

What is being drawn to our attention here is the fluid, constituted, plural and potentially, if not actually, contested character of 'imagined' social worlds.

The five dimensions identified need relatively little explanation. Ethnoscapes refer to the socio-spatial maps of mobile persons – 'tourists, immigrants, refugees, exiles, guestworkers' etc. – and allow us to recognise that our notions of space, place, and community have become much more complex, indeed a 'single community' may now be dispersed across a variety of sites (Rouse 1991). 'Technoscapes' alert us to the complex changing features of the global distribution of technologies, to the fact that it is not so much 'economies of scale . . . political control or . . . market rationality, but . . . increasingly complex relationships between money flows, political possibilities and the availability of both low and highly-skilled labour' (Appadurai 1990: 297–8) that affects the global configuration. 'Finanscapes' refer to the complex and fluctuating patterns assumed by global capital as it flows rapidly across the currency markets and stock exchanges of the world. And 'mediascapes' and 'ideoscapes' refer respectively to the capacity to produce and distribute information electronically, as well as to the images of the world thereby disseminated, and to the political ideologies of social movements and nation-states.

Disjunctures between the disposition of global capital; the distribution and impact of complex technologies; the patterns of migration of populations and associated transformations of both communities themselves and our sense of community; and the development of transnational media providing 'large and complex repertoires of images, narratives and "ethnoscapes" to viewers throughout the world, in which the world of commodities and the world of "news" and politics are profoundly mixed' (Appadurai 1990: 299), have already been identified by a number of analysts as conditioning the emergence of postmodernity (Lash and Urry 1987; Harvey 1989; Smart 1992). But it is perhaps in relation to ideoscapes that the relationship between globalisation and postmodernity becomes most apparent. Modern political ideologies developed in both Europe and America around or in response to the master narratives of the Enlightenment (i.e. freedom, sovereignty, representation, democracy, etc.). However, with the global diffusion or scattering of modernity the 'internal coherence which held these terms and images together in a Euro-American master-narrative' (Appadurai 1990: 300) has been dissipated. Indeed reference to the global diffusion of modern institutions and practices is itself potentially misleading, for it suggests a singular virtually uniform process, whereas in actuality the diffusion of modernity has been 'multi-dimensional and multi-directional', subject to an important degree to the rich diversity of cultural traditions, to 'changing forms of dependence on non-modern bases and forces of development' (Arnason 1990: 221). One implication of this is that modern political narratives are subject to (re)interpretation and reconstitution as they pass from context to context during processes of global diffusion. Another noted by Appadurai is that both the 'communicative genres' that are valued and the 'pragmatic genre conventions' governing the reception of political texts may vary significantly. For example 'democracy' may have become a virtually universal figure within both the legitimatory narratives of nation-states and the counter-discourses constituted by oppositional social and political movements, but the particular contextual conventions that predominate, the communicative genres that are privileged and the pragmatic genre conventions that regulate interpretations of political texts, effectively ensure that democracy is constituted in a diversity of forms. As Appadurai suggests, whilst ' "democracy" has clearly become a master-term with powerful echoes from Haiti and Poland to the Soviet Union and China . . . it sits at the center of a variety of ideoscapes (composed of distinctive pragmatic configurations of rough "translations" of other central terms from the vocabulary of the Enlightenment)' (1990: 301). A variety of ideoscapes that cannot be reduced to or accommodated within a singular grand political narrative. It is the implied recognition of the 'decline in the great myths of emancipation, universality and rationality' (Laclau 1990: 216) and the corollary, an acceptance of the plurality of cultures and discourses, that have been increasingly identified with the idea of a postmodern political condition.

As the scale, velocity and volume of global flows have increased so the associated disjunctures have become more fluid and uncertain. But if an increase in global flows has contributed to the 'deterritorialisation' of populations, commodities, money, images and ideas, the consequence has not so much been in the direction of cultural homogenisation as the reconstitution or regeneration of differences in and through displacement. For, as Appadurai concludes,

> globalisation involves the use of a variety of instruments of homogenisation . . . which are absorbed into local political and cultural economies, only to be repatriated as heterogeneous dialogues of national sovereignty, free enterprise, fundamentalism etc . . . The critical point is that both sides of the coin of global cultural process today are products of the infinitely varied mutual contest of sameness and difference on a stage characterised by radical disjunctures between different sorts of global flows and the uncertain landscapes erected in and through these disjunctions.
>
> (1990: 307–8)

It is in this global context where modern universalising tendencies associated with Western culture have been increasingly subject to reinterpretation, modification, transformation, and challenge, in short qualification if not particularisation, that a concept of postmodernity has been invoked.

Just as the modern quest for an orderly and certain world called into existence forms of disorder and uncertainty, so the global diffusion of modern Western economic, political and cultural forms of life has precipitated complex accommodations, adaptations, contests and conflicts between the 'same' and the 'different'. It is to this unpredictable and uncertain global condition that the idea of postmodernity belongs.

CONCLUDING REMARKS

Postmodernity remains a contentious term, signifying for some analysts simply a 'symptom of the current mood of the Western intelligentsia' (Callinicos 1989: 9), whilst for others it describes important aspects of the social, cultural and political conditions to which we increasingly find ourselves subject (Harvey 1989; Bauman 1992). And of those analysts who regard the term as appropriate for describing contemporary conditions some at least clearly consider the constituency affected, the 'we', not to be confined to either the 'first' world or the intelligentsia alone (Rouse 1991).

As I have attempted to make clear, discussion of the idea of postmodernity arises in the light (and shadow) of modernity and needs to be explored in relation to its complex and uneven consequences. In an age in which the world has been pictured increasingly as a 'single place', as a whole, reference has been made to both a pervasive process of 'Europeanisation' and subsequently to what is frequently represented as an even more extensive global process of 'Americanization'. And it is here in the context of a range of complex cultural exchanges and interrelationships between Europe and America that different aspects of the postmodern configuration receive their initial articulation (Calinescu 1977; Huyssen 1984; Smart 1990). The depth of contemporary interest in the idea of postmodernity arises in substantial part from the fact that the universal significance once accorded to goals and values articulated in 'Euro-American' master narratives and equated with modern Western civilisation no longer seems so persuasive. The very idea of modernity as a project associated with the West is in question, in one respect because the project itself remains incomplete or subject to doubt and challenge, and in another because modernity is increasingly recognised to be 'multi-dimensional and multi-directional' (Arnason 1990: 227), its complex articulations with pre-modern or traditional forms of sociality giving rise to a plurality of interconnected local and global transformations, transformations which extend in their diversity from 'intimate aspects of personal life . . . to the establishment of social connections of very wide scope' (Giddens 1991: 32).

For example, Western modernity (its institutional dimensions, developmental directions, and social consequences) has been challenged by the resurgence of Islam. Indeed, it might be argued that Islam has become the main counter-force to modern Western civilisation. But this does not necessarily mean that all aspects of modernity have been rejected, although the regeneration of traditional practices and institutions and the re-affirmation of religious faith in the face of modern secularity may convey that impression. Rather, given tradition is being 'affirmed *anew*, after an interval when it was *not* affirmed' (Berger 1980: 62), that is in a context where significant features of modernity have already been embedded in social processes, and indigenised within everyday social life, what we may be witnessing is not so much a fundamental rejection of modernity as a condemnation and rejection of the process of 'cultural Westernisation' which has frequently been articulated with it, if not the bearer of it. To what extent the regeneration of Islam and its corollary, the turn away from Western modernity, contributes to what has been termed the condition of postmodernity awaits further clarification (Ahmed 1992; Gellner 1992).

The configuration of Western modernity has been placed in question and challenged in a second, somewhat different manner by increasing evidence that the economic and cultural momentum has swung away from both Europe and America towards the Pacific rim and the modernising societies of the East. With the growing prominence of Japan and the possibility that its successful modernisation and increasing economic hegemony have been achieved without cultural Westernisation 'what were once assumed to be the universal cultural centres of the world . . . are . . . increasingly seen merely as centres of the limited Western project of modernity' (Featherstone 1991: 147). The idea of a universal project of modernity becomes difficult to sustain in these circumstances, particularly as the 'specific – and highly dynamic – constellation of economic, political and cultural determinants sets the Japanese road to modernity apart and relativises all parallels with earlier or more frequent patterns' (Arnason 1987/1988: 59).[4] The rapid achievement of an economically modern form of life through the promotion of capitalism and perpetuation of paternalist authoritarianism in other societies in South-East Asia, notably the 'Four Tigers' of Hong Kong, Singapore, South Korea and Taiwan, lends further weight to the argument that modernity is multi-dimensional and multi-directional.

It is in this context of a recognition of the openness of modernity, the diversity of configurations that may be articulated with it, and the realisation that there are other increasingly powerful non-Western civilisations exercising a globally extensive and growing influence over economic, cultural and political life, that a notion of *post*modernity has been invoked. A notion that suggests not the passing of modernity, not the end of history or politics, nor a nostalgic retrieval of a valued past, but a different way of relating to modern conditions and their consequences, to present circumstances and future prospects.

NOTES

[1] As Giddens remarks,

> Wallerstein successfully breaks away from some of the limitations of much orthodox sociological thought . . . But his work has its own shortcomings. He continues to see only one dominant institutional nexus (capitalism) as responsible for modern transformations. World-system theory thus concentrates heavily upon economic influences and finds it difficult satisfactorily to account for . . . the rise of the nation-state and the nation-state system . . . [and] to illuminate political or military concentrations of power, which do not align in an exact way to economic differentiations.
>
> (1990: 69)

[2] The other structural problems identified by Bell include the 'double bind' confronting the state as it seeks both to provide the necessary conditions for capital accumulation and meet 'the rising claims of citizens for income security, social services, social amenities and the like' (Bell 1980: 215). A double-bind which 'manifests itself in the fact that inflation or unemployment has become the virtual trade off of government policy, and governments are in the difficult position of constantly redefining what is an "acceptable" level of unemployment and an "acceptable" level of inflation' (1980: 217). Increasing levels of internal and external national debt and associated pressures towards economic nationalism and protectionism add to the problem, as do significant increases in the proportion of young people eligible to enter education and the labour market in less developed countries, countries already facing high levels of unemployment and underemployment. Where Bell asks will the "surplus" populations of the developing world go in the coming years?' (1980: 219). Finally there is the growing disparity between 'rich and poor nations', rising levels of poverty and a continuing absence in the developed world of the political will to move towards 'substantial income redistribution' (1980: 222–3).

[3] As one analyst comments, 'political absorption into the inter-national arena in terms of exchanging ambassadors, voting at the United Nations, expressing opinions on diplomatic issues of the day, is almost universal. How far a country permits itself to be absorbed into the world economy or to be conquered by the dominant culture nevertheless remains something which betrays considerable variation in the world' (Mazrui 1990: 239).

[4] The idea that Japan cannot be satisfactorily accommodated within a universalising model of modernity is broached by both Durkheim (1964: 88, n10) and Kojève (1969: 159–62, note to the second edition). In an edited collection on *Postmodernism and Japan* Miyoshi and Harootunian suggest that Kojève's comments anticipate aspects of the contemporary interest in 'the scene of Japan's postmodernity' (1989: xii). For further comment see Woodiwiss (1991) and Smart (1993).

References

Ahmed, A (1992), *Postmodernism and Islam: Predicament and Promise*, London, Routledge.

Ahmed, A (1990), 'Exorcising the Demon Image', *Guardian*, July 28.

Albrow, M (1990), 'Globalisation, Knowledge and Society: Introduction', in M Albrow and E King (eds), *Globalisation, Knowledge and Society*, London, Sage.

Alexander, J (1991), 'Understanding Social Science: Giving Up the Positivist Ghost', *Perspectives*, Volume 14, Number 1.

Anderson, B (1983), *Imagined Communities: Reflections on the Origin and Spread of Nationalism*, London, Verso.

Appadurai, A (1990), 'Disjuncture and Difference in the Global Cultural Economy', *Theory, Culture and Society*, Volume 7, Numbers 2 and 3.

Archer, M (1990), 'Foreword', in M Albrow and E King (eds), *Globalisation, Knowledge and Society*, London, Sage.

Arnason, J (1990), 'Nationalism, Globalisation and Modernity', *Theory, Culture and Society*, Volume 7, Numbers 2 and 3.

Arnason, J (1987/1988), 'The Modern Constellation and the Japanese Enigma – Part II', *Thesis Eleven*, Number 18/19.

Aronowitz, S (1987/1988), 'Postmodernism and Politics', *Social Text*, 18.

Bahro, R (1978), *The Alternative in Eastern Europe*, London, New Left Books.

Bataille, G (1983), *Story of the Eye*, Harmondsworth, Penguin.

Baudrillard, J (1990), *Fatal Strategies*, London, Semiotext(e)/ Pluto.

Baudrillard, J (1988d), *The Ecstasy of Communication*, New York, Semiotext(e).

Baudrillard, J (1988c), *America*, London, Verso.

Baudrillard, J (1988b), 'The Year 2000 Has Already Happened', in A and M Kroker (eds), *Body Invaders: Sexuality and the Postmodern Condition*, London, Macmillan.

Baudrillard, J (1988a), *The Evil Demon of Images*, Sydney, Power Institute Publications, Number 3.

Baudrillard, J (1987), *Forget Foucault and Forget Baudrillard*, New York, Semiotext(e).

Baudrillard, J (1984), 'Game with Vestiges', *On the Beach*, 5, Winter.

Baudrillard, J (1983b), *In the Shadow of the Silent Majorities . . . or The End of the Social and Other Essays*, New York, Semiotext(e).

Baudrillard, J (1983a), *Simulations*, New York, Semiotext(e).

Bauman, Z (1992), *Intimations of Postmodernity*, London, Routledge.

Bauman, Z (1991b), 'A Sociological Theory of Postmodernity', *Thesis Eleven*, 29.

Bauman, Z (1991a), *Modernity and Ambivalence*, Cambridge, Polity Press.

Bauman, Z (1990b), 'Effacing the Face: On the Social Management of Moral Proximity', *Theory, Culture and Society*, Volume 7, Number 1.

Bauman, Z (1990a), 'Philosophical Affinities of Postmodern Sociology', *Sociological Review*, Volume 38, Number 3.

Bauman, Z (1989), 'Sociological Responses to Postmodernity', *Thesis Eleven*, Number 23.

Bauman, Z (1988b), 'Sociology and Postmodernity', *Sociological Review*, Volume 36, Number 4.

Bauman, Z (1988a), 'Is There a Postmodern Sociology?', *Theory, Culture and Society*, Volume 5, Numbers 2 and 3.

Bauman, Z (1987), *Legislators and Interpreters: On Modernity, Postmodernity, and Intellectuals*, Cambridge, Polity Press.

Bell, D (1980), *Sociological Journeys: Essays 1960–1980*, London, Heinemann.

Bell, D (1976), *The Cultural Contradictions of Capitalism*, New York, Basic Books.

Bell, D (1973), *The Coming of Post-Industrial Society; A Venture in Social Forecasting*, New York, Basic Books.

Benjamin, A (ed.) (1989), *The Lyotard Reader*, Oxford, Blackwell.

Berger, P (1980), *The Heretical Imperative: Contemporary Possibilities of Religious Affirmation*, New York, Doubleday.

Berger, P, Berger, B and Kellner, H (1973), *The Homeless Mind: Modernization and Consciousness*, New York, Random House.

Berger, P and Luckmann, T (1975), *The Social Construction of Reality*, Harmondsworth, Penguin.

Berman, M (1985), *All That is Solid Melts Into Air: The Experience of Modernity*, London, Verso.

Bhaba, H (1989), 'World Writer's Statement', in L Appignanesi and S Maitland (eds), *The Rushdie File*, London, Fourth Estate.

Bhaba, H and Parekh, B (1989), 'Identities on Parade: A Conversation', *Marxism Today*, June.

Bierstedt, R (1979), 'Sociological Thought in the Eighteenth Century' in T Bottomore and R Nisbet (eds), *A History of Sociological Analysis*, London, Heinemann.

Block, F (1990), *Postindustrial Possibilities: A Critique of Economic Discourse*, Oxford, University of California Press.

Bock, K (1979), 'Theories of Progress, Development, Evolution' in T Bottomore and R Nisbet (eds), *A History of Sociological Analysis*, London, Heinemann.

Bottomore, T and Nisbet, R (eds) (1979), *A History of Sociological Analysis*, London, Heinemann.

Boyne, R and Rattansi, A (eds) (1990), *Postmodernism and Society*, London, Macmillan.

Burgin, V (1986), *The End of Art Theory: Criticism and Postmodernity*, London, Macmillan.

Calinescu, M (1977), *Faces of Modernity*, London, Indiana University Press.

Callinicos, A (1991), *The Revenge of History: Marxism and the East European Revolutions*, Cambridge, Polity Press.

Callinicos, A (1990), 'Reactionary Postmodernism?', in R Boyne and A Rattansi (eds), *Postmodernism and Society*, London, Macmillan.

Callinicos, A (1989), *Against Postmodernism: A Marxist Critique*, Cambridge, Polity Press.

Castells, M (1989), *The Informational City*, Oxford, Blackwell.

Chen, K H (1987), 'The Masses and the Media: Baudrillard's Implosive Postmodernism', *Theory, Culture and Society*, Volume 4, Number 1.

Chomsky, N (1991), 'The Weak Shall Inherit Nothing', *Guardian Weekly*, Volume 144, Number 14.

Dallmayr, F (1982), 'The Theory of Structuration: a Critique', in A Giddens (1982) *Profiles and Critiques in Social Theory*, London, Macmillan.

Dawe, A (1979), 'Theories of Social Action', in T Bottomore and R Nisbet (eds), *A History of Sociological Analysis*, London, Heinemann.

Dews, P (1987), *Logics of Disintegration: Post-structuralist Thought and the Claims of Critical Theory*, London, Verso.

Donzelot, J (1988), 'The Promotion of the Social', *Economy and Society*, Volume 17, Number 3.

Donzelot, J (1979), 'The Poverty of Political Culture', *Ideology and Consciousness*, Number 5.

Dreyfus, H and Rabinow, P (1986), 'What is Maturity? Habermas and Foucault on "What is Enlightenment" ', in D C Hoy (ed), *Foucault: A Critical Reader*, Oxford, Blackwell.

Dreyfus, H L and Rabinow, P (1982), *Michel Foucault: Beyond Structuralism and Hermeneutics*, Sussex, Harvester Press.

Durkheim, E (1964), *The Rules of Sociological Method*, New York, Free Press.

Eco, U (1989), *Foucault's Pendulum*, London, Secker and Warburg.

Eco, U (1987), *Travels in Hyperreality*, London, Picador.

Eco, U (1984), *The Name of the Rose*, London, Picador.

Eco, U (1978), 'Silence is L(e)aden', in P Foss and M Morris (eds), *Language, Sexuality and Subversion*, Sydney, Feral Publications.

Featherstone, M (1991), *Consumer Culture and Postmodernism*, London, Sage.

Featherstone, M (1990), 'Global Culture: An Introduction', *Theory, Culture and Society*, Volume 7, Numbers 2 and 3.

Featherstone, M (1988), 'In Pursuit of the Postmodern: An Introduction', *Theory, Culture and Society*, Volume 5, Numbers
2 and 3.

Fekete, J (1988), *Life After Postmodernism: Essays on Value
and Culture*, London, Macmillan.

Feyerabend, P (1975), *Against Method*, London, New Left
Books.

Focillon, H (1970), *The Year 1000*, New York, F Ungar Publication Co.

Foster, H (ed.) (1985), *Postmodern Culture*, London, Pluto
Press.

Foucault, M (1986c), 'Preface to *The History of Sexuality*,
Volume II' in P Rabinow (ed.), *The Foucault Reader*, Harmondsworth, Penguin Books.

Foucault, M (1986b), 'Kant on Enlightenment and Revolution',
Economy and Society, Volume 15, Number 1.

Foucault, M (1986a), 'What is Enlightenment?', in P Rabinow
(ed.), *The Foucault Reader*, Harmondsworth, Penguin
Books.

Foucault, M (1982b), 'Is it Really Important to Think?', *Philosophy and Social Criticism*, Volume 9, Number 1.

Foucault, M (1982a), 'Space, Knowledge and Power: An Interview', *Skyline*, March.

Foucault, M (1981), 'Questions of Method: An Interview', *I and
C*, Number 8.

Foucault, M (1980), *Power/Knowledge – Selected Interviews and
Other Writings 1972–1977*, ed. C Gordon, Brighton, Harvester Press.

Foucault, M (1978), 'Introduction' to G Canguilhem, *On the
Normal and the Pathological*, London, D Reidel.

Foucault, M (1977b), *Discipline and Punish: The Birth of the
Prison*, London, Allen Lane.

Foucault, M (1977a), *Language, Counter-Memory, Practice:
Selected Essays and Interviews*, ed. D F Bouchard, Oxford,
Blackwell.

Foucault, M (1973), *The Order of Things: An Archaeology of
the Human Sciences*, New York, Vintage Books.

Frankel, B (1987), *The Post-Industrial Utopians*, Cambridge,
Polity Press.

Friedman, J (1990), 'Being in the World: Globalization and
Localization', *Theory, Culture and Society*, Volume 7, Numbers 2 and 3.

Fukuyama, F (1989), 'The End of History?', *The National Interest*, 16.

Furbank, P N (1988), 'A Definite Article Debagged', *The Times Higher Education Supplement*, Number 839.

Geras, N (1987), 'Post-Marxism?', *New Left Review*, 187.

Gellner, E (1992), *Postmodernism, Reason and Religion*, London, Routledge.

Gellner, E (1988), *Plough, Sword and Book: The Structure of Human History*, London, Collins Harvill.

Giddens, A (1991), *Modernity and Self-Identity*, Cambridge, Polity Press.

Giddens, A (1990), *The Consequences of Modernity*, Cambridge, Polity Press.

Giddens, A (1987), *Social Theory and Modern Sociology*, Cambridge, Polity Press.

Giddens, A (1985), *The Nation-State and Violence*, Cambridge, Polity Press.

Giddens, A (1984), *The Constitution of Society*, Cambridge, Polity Press.

Giddens, A (1982), *Profiles and Critiques in Social Theory*, London, Macmillan.

Giddens, A (1979), *Central Problems in Social Theory*, London, Macmillan.

Gordon, C (1987), 'The Soul of the Citizen: Max Weber and Michel Foucault on Rationality and Government', in S Whimster and S Lash (eds), *Max Weber, Rationality and Modernity*, London, Allen and Unwin.

Gorz, A (1982), *Farewell to the Working Class: An Essay on Post-Industrial Socialism*, London, Pluto Press.

Gouldner, A (1971), *The Coming Crisis of Western Sociology*, London, Heinemann.

Grossberg, L (1988), 'It's a Sin: Politics, Post-Modernity and the Popular', in L Grossberg (ed.), *It's a Sin : Essays on Postmodernism, Politics and Culture*, Sydney, Power Publications.

Habermas, J (1987), *The Theory of Communicative Action*, Volume 2, *Lifeworld and System: A Critique of Functionalist Reason*, Cambridge, Polity Press.

Habermas, J (1981), 'Modernity Versus Postmodernity', *New German Critique*, Number 22.

Hacking, I (1988), 'Night Thoughts on Philology', *History of the Present*, Number 4.

Hall, S (1977), 'Rethinking the "Base and Superstructure" metaphor', in J Bloomfield (ed.), *Class, Hegemony and Party*, London, Lawrence and Wishart.

Hannerz, U (1990), 'Cosmopolitans and Locals in World Culture', *Theory, Culture and Society*, Volume 7, Numbers 2 and 3.

Harvey, D (1989), *The Condition of Postmodernity*, London, Blackwell.

Haynor, A (1990), 'In Defence of Universal Theory', *Perspectives*, Volume 13, Number 4.

Hebblethwaite, P (1989), 'The Works of Satan', *Guardian Weekly*, Volume 140, Number 10.

Hebdige, D (1989), 'New Times: After the Masses', *Marxism Today*, January.

Hebdige, D (1988), *Hiding in the Light: On Images and Things*, London, Routledge.

Heidegger, M (1977), *The Question Concerning Technology and Other Essays*, London, Garland Publishing Inc.

Heidegger, M (1971), *On the Way to Language*, London, Harper and Row.

Hekman, S (1990), *Gender and Knowledge: Elements of a Postmodern Feminism*, Cambridge, Polity Press.

Heller, A (1990a) 'Death of the Subject', *Thesis Eleven*, Number 25.

Heller, A (1990b), *Can Modernity Survive?*, Cambridge, Polity Press.

Heller, A and Feher, F (1988), *The Postmodern Political Condition*, Cambridge, Polity Press.

Hennis, W (1988), *Max Weber: Essays in Reconstruction*, London, Allen and Unwin.

Hirst, P (1990), 'An Answer to Relativism?', *New Formations*, Spring.

Hirst, P and Woolley, P (1982), *Social Relations and Human Attributes*, London, Tavistock.

Hobsbawm, E and Ranger, T (eds) (1983), *The Invention of Tradition*, New York, Columbia University Press.

Hoy, D (1988), 'Foucault: Modern or Postmodern?', in J Arac (ed.), *After Foucault: Humanistic Knowledge, Postmodern Challenges*, London, Rutgers University Press.

Huyssen, A (1984), 'Mapping the Postmodern', *New German Critique*, 33.

Illich, I (1978), *The Right to Useful Unemployment and its Pro-fessional Enemies*, London, Marion Boyars.

Jameson, F (1991), *Postmodernism or The Cultural Logic of Late Capitalism*, London, Verso.

Jameson, F (1989), 'Marxism and Postmodernism', *New Left Review*, Number 176.

Jameson, F (1988), 'Cognitive Mapping', in C Nelson and L Grossberg (eds), *Marxism and the Interpretation of Culture*, London, Macmillan.

Jameson, F (1984), 'Postmodernism or the Cultural Logic of Late Capitalism', *New Left Review*, Number 146.

Jay, M (1988), *Fin-De-Siècle Socialism: And Other Essays*, London, Routledge.

Kant, I (1963), *On History*, ed L W Beck, New York, Bobbs Merrill.

Kellner, D (1988), 'Postmodernism as Social Theory: Some Chal-lenges and Problems', *Theory, Culture and Society*, Volume 5, Numbers 2 and 3.

Kojève, A (1969), *Introduction to the Reading of Hegel*, London, Basic Books, Inc.

Kroker, A and Cook, D (1988), *The Postmodern Scene: Excre-mental Culture and Hyper-Aesthetics*, London, Macmillan.

Kumar, K (1988), *The Rise of Modern Society: Aspects of the Social and Political Development of the West*, Oxford, Blackwell.

Laclau, E (1990), *New Reflections on the Revolution of Our Time*, London, Verso.

Laclau, E (1988), 'Politics and the Limits of Modernity', in A Ross (ed.), *Universal Abandon? The Politics of Postmodern-ism*, Minneapolis, University of Minnesota Press.

Laclau, E and Mouffe, C (1987), 'Post-Marxism Without Apolo-gies', *New Left Review*, 166.

Laclau, E and Mouffe, C (1985), *Hegemony and Socialist Strat-egy*, London, Verso.

Lash, S (1990), *Sociology of Postmodernism*, London, Rout-ledge.

Lash, S and Urry, J (1987), *The End of Organized Capitalism*, Cambridge, Polity Press.

Levin, D M (1988), *The Opening of Vision: Nihilism and the Postmodern Situation*, London, Routledge.

Lyotard, J F (1989), 'Complexity and the Sublime', in L Appignanesi (ed.), *Postmodernism*, ICA Documents, London, Free Association Books.

Lyotard, J F (1988b), 'An Interview', *Theory, Culture and Society*, Volume 5, Numbers 2 and 3.

Lyotard, J F (1988a), *The Differend: Phrases in Dispute*, Manchester, Manchester University Press.

Lyotard, J F (1986), *The Postmodern Condition: A Report on Knowledge*, Manchester, Manchester University Press.

McCarthy, T (1984), 'Translators Introduction' to J Habermas, *The Theory of Communicative Action*, Volume One, *Reason and the Rationalisation of Society*, London, Heinemann.

Macintyre, A (1982), *After Virtue: A Study in Moral Theory*, London, Duckworth.

McRobbie, A (1991), 'New Times in Cultural Studies', *New Formations*, Number 13, Spring.

Maffesoli, M (1990), 'Post-Modern Sociality', *Telos*, 35.

Mandel, E (1980), *Late Capitalism*, London, Verso.

Marx, K and Engels, F (1968), *The Communist Manifesto*, Harmondsworth, Penguin.

Mazrui, A A (1990), *Cultural Forces in World Politics*, London, James Currey.

Merquior, J G (1985), *Foucault*, London, Fontana.

Mestrovic, S (1991), *The Coming Fin De Siècle: An Application of Durkheim's Sociology to Modernity and Postmodernism*, London, Routledge.

Miyoshi, M and Harootunian, H D (eds) (1989), *Postmodernism and Japan*, London, Duke University Press.

Mommsen, W (1987), 'Personal Conduct and Societal Change', in S Whimster and S Lash (eds), *Max Weber, Rationality and Modernity*, London, Allen and Unwin.

Morris, M (1988), *The Pirate's Fiancée: Feminism, Reading, Postmodernism*, London, Verso.

Newman, M (1989), 'Revising Modernism, Representing Postmodernism: Critical Discourses of the Visual Arts', in L Appignanesi (ed.), *Postmodernism*, ICA Documents, London, Free Association Books.

Nietzsche, F (1978), *Beyond Good and Evil: Prelude to a Philosophy of the Future*, Harmondsworth, Penguin.

Nietzsche, F (1969), *On the Genealogy of Morals*, New York, Vintage Books.

Nietszche, F (1968), *The Will to Power*, New York, Vintage Books.

Noble, D (1984), *Forces of Production: A Social History of Industrial Automation*, New York, A Knopf.

Poster, M (1990), *The Mode of Information: Poststructuralism and Social Context*, Cambridge, Polity Press.

Rabinow, P (1986), 'Representations Are Social Facts: Modernity and Post-Modernity in Anthropology', in J Clifford and G E Marcus (eds), *Writing Culture: The Poetics and Politics of Ethnography*, London, University of California Press.

Rajchman, J (1985), *Michel Foucault: The Freedom of Philosophy*, New York, Columbia University Press.

Robertson, R (1990), 'Mapping the Global Condition: Globalization as the Central Concept', *Theory, Culture and Society*, Volume 7, Numbers 2 and 3.

Robertson, R and Lechner, F (1985), 'Modernization, Globalisation and the Problem of Culture in World-Systems Theory', *Theory, Culture and Society*, Volume 2, Number 3.

Rorty, R (1989), *Contingency, Irony and Solidarity*, Cambridge, Cambridge University Press.

Rorty, R (1979), *Philosophy and the Mirror of Nature*, Princeton, Princeton University Press.

Roth, G (1987), 'Rationalisation in Max Weber's Developmental History', in S Whimster and S Lash (eds), *Max Weber, Rationality and Modernity*, London, Allen and Unwin.

Rouse, R (1991), 'Mexican Migration and the Social Space of Postmodernism', *Diaspora*, Volume 1, Number 1.

Rushdie, S (1989), 'Bonfire of the Certainties', *Guardian Weekly*, Volume 140, Number 9.

Rushdie, S (1988), *The Satanic Verses*, London, Viking.

Ryan, M (1988), 'Postmodern Politics', *Theory, Culture and Society*, Volume 5, Numbers 2 and 3.

Sacks, J (1991), *The Persistence of Faith*, London, Weidenfeld and Nicolson.

Said, E (1989), 'Dealing with Rushdie's "Complicated Mixture" ', *Guardian Weekly*, Volume 140, Number 12.

Sawicki, J (1988), 'Feminism and the Power of Foucaldian Discourse', in J Arac (ed.), *After Foucault: Humanistic Knowledge, Postmodern Challenges*, London, Rutgers University Press.

Sayer, D (1991), *Capitalism and Modernity: An Excursus on Marx and Weber*, London, Routledge.

Seidman, S (1990), 'Against Theory as a Foundationalist Discourse', *Perspectives*, Volume 13, Number 2.

Smart, B (1993), 'Europe/America : Baudrillard's Fatal Comparison', in C Rojek and B Turner (eds), *Forget Baudrillard?*, London, Routledge.

Smart, B (1992), *Modern Conditions, Postmodern Controversies*, London, Routledge.

Smart, B (1990), 'Modernity, Postmodernity and the Present' in B Turner (ed.), *Theories of Modernity and Postmodernity*, London, Sage.

Smart, B (1986), 'The Politics of Truth and the Problem of Hegemony', in D C Hoy (ed.), *Foucault: A Critical Reader*, Oxford, Blackwell.

Smart, B (1985), *Michel Foucault*, London, Routledge.

Smith, A D (1990), 'Towards a Global Culture?', *Theory, Culture and Society*, Volume 7, Numbers 2 and 3.

Soja, E W (1989), *Postmodern Geographies: The Reassertion of Space in Critical Social Theory*, London, Verso.

Sommer, T (1991), 'A World Beyond Order and Control', *Guardian Weekly*, Volume 144, Number 17.

Tenbruck, F H (1990), 'The Dream of a Secular Ecumene: The Meaning and Limits of Policies of Development', *Theory, Culture and Society*, Volume 7, Numbers 2 and 3.

Therborn, G (1989), 'New Times: Vorsprung Durch Rethink', *Marxism Today*, February.

Tololyan, K (1991), 'The Nation-State and Its Other: In Lieu of a Preface', *Diaspora*, Volume 1, Number 1.

Touraine, A (1989), 'Is Sociology Still the Study of Society?', *Thesis Eleven*, Number 23.

Touraine, A (1984), 'The Waning Sociological Image of Social Life', *International Journal of Comparative Sociology*, Volume 25, Numbers 1 and 2.

Toynbee, A (1954b), *A Study of History*, Volume 9, London, Oxford University Press.

Toynbee, A (1954a), *A Study of History*, Volume 8, London, Oxford University Press.

Turner, B (ed.) (1990), *Theories of Modernity and Postmodernity*, London, Sage.

Tyler, S A (1986), 'Post-Modern Ethnography: From Document of the Occult to Occult Document', in J Clifford and G E Marcus (eds), *Writing Culture: The Poetics and Politics of Ethnography*, London, University of California Press.

Vattimo, G (1988), *The End of Modernity*, Cambridge, Polity Press.

Veerman, D (1988), 'Introduction to Lyotard', *Theory, Culture and Society*, Volume 5, Numbers 2 and 3.

Wallace, W (1991), 'Standardizing Basic Sociological Concepts', *Perspectives*, Volume 14, Number 1.

Wallerstein, I (1990), 'Culture as the Ideological Battleground of the Modern World-System', *Theory, Culture and Society*, Volume 7, Numbers 2 and 3.

Wark, M (1990), 'The Tyranny of Difference', *Tension*, 23.

Weber, M (1970), *From Max Weber: Essays in Sociology*, eds H H Gerth and C Wright Mills, London, Routledge and Kegan Paul.

Weiss, J (1987), 'On the Irreversibility of Western Rationalisation and Max Weber's Alleged Fatalism', in S Whimster and S Lash (eds), *Max Weber, Rationality and Modernity*, London, Allen and Unwin.

Whimster, S and Lash, S (eds) (1987), *Max Weber, Rationality and Modernity*, London, Allen and Unwin.

Wolff, K (1989), 'From Nothing to Sociology', *Philosophy of the Social Sciences*, Volume 19, Number 3.

Woodiwiss, A. (1991), '*Postmodanizumu*: Japanese For (and Against) Postmodernism', *Theory, Culture and Society*, Volume 8, Number 4.

Worsley, P (1990), 'Models of the Modern World System', *Theory, Culture and Society*, Volume 7, Numbers 2 and 3.

Wright Mills, C (1970), *The Sociological Imagination*, Harmondsworth, Penguin.

Name index

Subject index